The
BORDER COLLIE

EDITED BY
JUDITH GREGORY

BEST of
BREED

ACKNOWLEDGEMENTS

The publishers would like to acknowledge the following for help with photography: Judith Gregory (Tonkory); Sue Ader (Passim); Maggie Peacock (Arnpriors); John and Sue Gifford (Brueway); Hearing Dogs for Deaf People and Pets As Therapy. Special thanks to Rosey Durrant (Rosmarinus) and the Lake District Sheep Dog Experience (www.lakedistrictsheepdogexperience.co.uk) for the use of their beautiful photographs, and Andrew Hall of the Working Sheepdog Archive for help with historical photographs.

Cover photo: © Tracy Morgan Animal Photography (www.animalphotographer.co.uk)
page 8 © istockphoto.com/Robert Churchill

The British Breed Standard reproduced in Chapter 7 is the copyright of the Kennel Club and published with the club's kind permission. Extracts from the American Breed Standard are reproduced by kind permission of the American Kennel Club.

THE QUESTION OF GENDER
The 'he' pronoun is used throughout this book instead of the rather impersonal 'it',
but no gender bias is intended.

First published in 2009 by The Pet Book Publishing Company Limited
Chepstow, NP16 7LG, UK.

This edition published in 2010. Reprinted in 2012.

ISBN
978-1-906305-18-5
1-906305-18-8

Printed and bound in China through Printworks Int. Ltd.

CONTENTS

GETTING TO KNOW BORDER COLLIES

Chapter 1

The Border Collie – just the mention of that name sends a shiver of excitement through my body and that is why I have owned, worked and bred them for nearly 50 years. The origin of the word 'collie' is thought to be the old Celtic word for 'useful' - and that is exactly what he is. He was originally bred to herd, drive and guard flocks of sheep and other livestock and that instinct can be channelled into Obedience, Agility, Working Trials and running smoothly around a breed show ring.

The Border Collie is extremely loyal and very biddable, but in the wrong hands he can become very naughty if he is not given the decisive leadership he requires. Prospective buyers of puppies say: "I want one that will be like the Border Collies on One Man and His Dog" – the television series which features sheepdog trials. But people do not realise that it takes many hours of training, good discipline, patience and a superb sense of timing to get a dog to that standard. Recently television entertainment programmes have featured Border Collies dancing and doing Heelwork to Music and viewers have been impressed by the close relationship between the handler and the dog, especially when the handler is a young teenage girl. This tends to increase the popularity of the breed, which is sometimes good and sometimes not so good.

Over many years of breeding, I have realised that once someone has owned a Border Collie then they never want any other breed. The average life span of a Border Collie is between 12 and 16 years and therefore, they are with the person for a large part of their life. As a practising psychotherapist and a breeder of Border Collies, I know how devastating the loss of dog can be and what far reaching effects it has on a person's life and relationships if the dog is not grieved for properly. Some people say: "It's only a dog", but 'it' is a being that has given unconditional love and been a constant companion for many years. In fact, one of the most outstanding characteristics of the Border Collie is his love of human companionship and his desire to follow you around wherever you go – even to the toilet if he can. You will always know where the owner of a Border Collie is as you will see him patiently waiting outside a door.

Border Collies are workaholics and therefore, they need to be stimulated. They can make excellent companion dogs, but still need to be taught basic

Born to herd: The Border Collie working in his traditional role.

manners and maybe tricks, which they love doing and learn very quickly. This is truly a unique breed whose intelligence and desire to work makes him the most versatile dog in the world.

PHYSICAL CHARACTERISTICS

The Border Collie is a medium-sized dog with a smooth, medium or heavy rough coat. He comes in a variety of colours and is athletic in appearance.

HEIGHT AND WEIGHT

The UK Kennel Club (KC) Standard states the ideal height for dogs is 21 inches (530 mm) and for bitches is 19 inches (480 mm), whereas the American KC gives ranges for dogs 19-22 inches (480- 560 mm) and for bitches 18- 21 inches (460- 530 mm).

An adult Border Collie weighs approximately 20 kg (44 lbs) and should be fit and well muscled. He should never be allowed to get overweight or fat, as this usually indicates lack of exercise or too many titbits.

COAT

The coat of a Border Collie is dense and double, with a thick short undercoat and a longer more weatherproof outer coat. This is to give protection when working in all weathers. Most of my dogs will quite happily stand out in rain and snow, even when they can take cover in a warm and wind/rain proof kennel. I have however, owned a Border Collie that never put a foot outside if it was raining, despite the fact that he had a profuse coat. Too much heat is not good for this breed and you will often see Border Collies that live in the house lying on cold tiles and in front of the door.

Most Border Collies live very happily outside and also love the comfort of a warm kitchen or bed by the Aga in the winter. If a dog is kennelled from the beginning he is used to that regime; if he is a house dog, he will not take kindly to being put outside for any length of time.

The Border Collie is a medium-sized, well-proportioned dog, with the stamina and agility to endure long periods of active work.

COLOUR

Border Collies come in variety of colours and the UK Kennel Club (KC) Standard allows any colour, as long as white does not predominate. This is because originally shepherds believed that sheep did not respect a white collie. Having said that, there were a great many top obedience dogs that were predominately white. The famous Ob. Ch. Fleet, Ob. Ch. Asa and Sylvia Bishop's 'Sunny' were very famous obedience dogs and distinct for the amount of white on them, as were many of the Shanvaal lines in obedience.

The most common colour is black and white followed by tan, black and white, which is commonly called tri-coloured. Red merles, blue merles, blue and white, red and white, Australian EE red, sable, and chocolate and white are all acceptable colours. At the Border Union Championship show on Saturday 14th of June 2008, the first blue merle Show Champion was made up, which was very exciting news for the breed. It is interesting to note that there is only one blue merle and one red merle Show Champion and they are both bitches.

Some years ago people were breeding lilac and white and pink and white and asking more money for them, claiming that they were 'rare'. Buyers should be wary of this claim and should be aware that these are dilute colours and no better or worse than any other colour of Border Collie. If someone is looking for a fashion accessory, they should not be looking for a Border Collie.

The Australian KC Breed Standard is more specific about the acceptable colours which it names as black and white, blue and white, chocolate and white, red and white, blue merle and tri-colours of black, tan and white. Sable or red merle is not acceptable. The Border Collie Breed Council was asked to look into this a couple of years ago and we decided after much discussion, to recommend that the KC should leave the UK Breed Standard as it stood regarding colour.

BORDER COLLIE COLOURS
This is a breed that comes in a wide variety of colours.

The classic black and white markings.

Tri colour: Black and white with tan markings.

Blue merle.

Red merle.

Blue and white.

Red and white.

Sable.

Blue sable.

11

This is a breed that requires regular free running exercise.

Some years ago, I was at the Border Collie Nationals, held at the Purina Farms in Louisville, USA. The event is run over a week with obedience, agility and herding competitions and culminates in two days of showing. There are also seminars on hereditary conditions and workshops for grooming and handling. One of the top bitches had a half white or split face. A half white faced dog would be very unlikely to be made into a Show Champion in the UK, despite the fact that there are some very nicely constructed Border Collies with half white faces. As a breeder, I sell puppies that have too much white or half white faces more cheaply, or they go to agility or obedience homes or as companion dogs.

In a series of television programmes presented by the well-known actor Martin Clunes, and his dogs, he was seen talking and working with a shepherd in Cumbria. The shepherd had two bitches, one was older and fully trained and a younger, smooth coated dog that was in training. They were both working the sheep with consummate ease. It was very interesting to note that the older dog was almost entirely white, except for a tri-coloured head, bearing in mind that it is a widely held opinion that shepherds believe that sheep do not respect a white dog. This example appeared to dispel this belief, but of course, it may have been in this case, that the sheep could only see the tri-coloured head pointing at them.

EXERCISE REQUIREMENTS

Adult Border Collies need a minimum of two 20 minute walks every day. This is an athletic breed and a Border Collie will become frustrated if he is not exercised regularly. He can be trained to trot along at the side of a bike on a safe cycle path, or there are many dog walking machines on the market that can be used in wet and muddy weather. However, this method should not be used to the exclusion of a good romp in the fields with lots of interesting smells and people and dogs to encounter.

The young Border Collie, under 12 months, should be exercised very carefully and not allowed free running with adult dogs. The period between 4 and

The Border Collie always has an independent mind but he has a special relationship with his owner.

12 months is a crucial time in the development of the bone and joint conformation. There is a growth spurt around five months, when the long bones are developing and the joints are forming. During this period, the puppy should be exercised on a lead and not allowed to jump or twist. Throwing frisbees and balls must be avoided at this time, as the dog can jump and twist and cause problems in the shoulders and hips which will present as lameness. This often occurs in multi-dog households where the dogs are run together.

If you have more than one Border Collie, care must be taken when throwing toys as Border Collies become excited and collisions can occur resulting in injuries or squabbles. A stick should never be used when playing with a Border Collie, even though he will enjoy bringing it back to you. A Border Collie is very fast and can run on to the stick and it can lodge in the dog's throat or go up into the roof of his mouth. I have personally had this experience and it is very frightening and distressing to the dog and the owner. This type of accident can end up with the dog bleeding or choking to death.

A fenced garden is essential for a Border Collie, where he can roam freely and safely. The Border Collie is best suited to country living, but will also live quite happily in a town house with a garden and some open space close by for his walks. I have noticed that dogs I have sold to people in urban areas seem to be better socialised and I often see them walking calmly round the shops or waiting patiently outside a shop in a down position for the return of their owner. I sold a puppy to a lady who has two adult Border Collies. She drives to a disused airfield at 6am and again in the evening for a good long run and the rest of the day, unless they are training, they lie contentedly in the house. Needless to say she does not let the puppy accompany her on these runs at this early stage.

When the dog becomes adult he should be allowed free running in fields, provided he is under control. He will also require roadwork on the lead to keep his feet in trim. When free

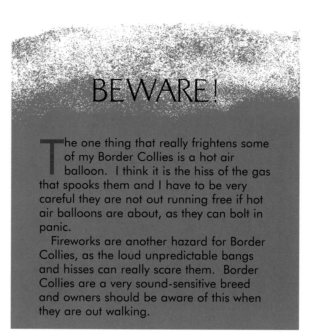

running a Border Collie, great care must be taken not to let an untrained dog loose if sheep or cattle are around, as their instinct is to round up, i.e. chase. Unless a Border Collie is properly trained, he should be kept on a lead. Some Border Collies will chase cars and bicycles, or in fact, anything that moves quickly. This behaviour needs to be eliminated with firm handling otherwise walks could become a nightmare (see Chapter 6: Training and Socialisation).

Most Border Collies love swimming in rivers or the sea and there are many kennels that now have hydrotherapy pools for the rehabilitation of dogs after injury or surgery. Swimming is very good for Border Collies, as the exercise can be enjoyable without putting pressure on young or injured joints. The movement will allow the muscles to strengthen and support the dog more easily.

TEMPERAMENT

The UK Kennel Club Breed Standard for the Border Collie states:

"The Border Collie should be keen, alert, responsive and intelligent. Neither nervous nor aggressive."

My own experience over the years has shown me that some Border Collies adore everyone

BEWARE!

The one thing that really frightens some of my Border Collies is a hot air balloon. I think it is the hiss of the gas that spooks them and I have to be very careful they are not out running free if hot air balloons are about, as they can bolt in panic.

Fireworks are another hazard for Border Collies, as the loud unpredictable bangs and hisses can really scare them. Border Collies are a very sound-sensitive breed and owners should be aware of this when they are out walking.

and want to go up and play with everyone and other dogs, whilst others are more reserved. They only want to be with their owners and are not bothered about other people. Whichever type a Border Collie is, he will always be loving and loyal to his owners.

When I was 15 years old, I used to spend a great deal of time on a sheep farm where a Border Collie would lie in the yard when he was not working. I was always told: "Don't touch the dog" and I had to restrain myself from making a fuss of him. The shepherd told me that the reason for this was that his Border Collie was for work and he did not want him distracted. Many farmers and shepherds thought this way and therefore, did not socialise their puppies.

Times have changed and most breeders believe in the importance of socialising puppies whether they are breeding for work, show or pet. Most of the show Border Collies get very used to being handled by the judge, being in a ring with other Border Collies and being on a busy show ground week after week from the age of six months, and they usually take it all in their stride.

Like most other breeders, I whelp puppies in the home before they go out to the puppy run and I put a lot of effort into socialising them so that they are used to people, household noises, going in cars, etc. My grandchildren, as did their parents before them, come to sit with the pups and pick them up as soon as the bitch is happy to let them.

It must be remembered that Border Collies were bred to be fast and use their initiative, e.g. nipping at the heels of stubborn sheep or cattle. This nipping can occasionally show itself in the interaction with siblings and other dogs. If the adult dogs or siblings do not deal with it, this behaviour must be stopped at an early stage with consistent, firm handling coupled with a distraction such as a toy or bone.

I often think certain types of

This is a breed that loves to learn. Teaching tricks is just one way of channelling a Border Collie's intelligence.

human temperament are suited to the Border Collie. Just like the Border Collie, the owner should be active and intelligent, decisive, firm and fun loving. If not properly socialised, some Border Collies are not suitable for families with small children, especially if they have not kept a dog before. The childrens' shrill voices and quick movements can be misunderstood by a young Border Collie.

I have always had Border Collies with my children and now grandchildren. When my son was young, he used to play football with our Border Collie and she would dribble the ball all round the pitch or stay in goal and leap into the air to save shots. The children loved her and as long as she did not puncture the ball, she was very popular.

TRAINABILITY

The Border Collie is probably the easiest dog to train because of his attentiveness and will to please. This is a very biddable breed and most Border Collies want to stay with their owners rather than being tempted to run off, which can be a problem with some of the hunting, scenting breeds. However, the Border Collie does have a strong chase instinct and this needs to be kept in check. I always tell puppy purchasers that the most important training is the 'instant down'. This gives control of the dog and it could be a life saver for the dog and maybe the owner as well.

Border Collies love to learn tricks such as high five, shake a paw, roll over and play dead – all these fun exercises can be taught to a young Border Collie in the

confines of the living room. You only have to watch Mary Ray with her Border Collies doing Heel Work to Music (HWTM), Agility or Obedience to see how her dogs love learning new tricks and performing what they have learned. Other breeds are certainly capable of doing HWTM, Agility and many of the other canine disciplines, but I think Border Collies demonstrate their joy and desire to do it and always want to do more.

This desire to work and play can become very wearing on less active people and, therefore, prospective owners must be made aware of what they are taking on. If the Border Collie is not taught the right way by skilful handling, he will be quick to learn the wrong way and then attempt to take over. This should

In time, a Border Collie will learn not to chase and will live in harmony with the family cat.

never be allowed to happen. However, most owners of Border Collies would never want another breed, and I get people coming back to me after 12 years or more, asking for another puppy when their first Border Collie has died.

LIVING WITH OTHER PETS

A new puppy should be introduced to existing dogs and other pets in the household carefully and slowly and always supervised in the early stages. An old dog may not welcome a new puppy into his territory at first. Gradually the pup, who is usually submissive, will learn his place in the pecking order and fall into line. In fact, I am often told by puppy buyers that the new pup gives the older dog a new lease of life.

A cat will usually find a way of putting a young puppy in his place by standing its ground and spitting or striking rapidly with a paw, initially with claws withdrawn. The puppy must be supervised, as he can be in danger of having his eyes scratched if he doesn't learn to back off pretty quickly. In time, the pair will learn to live in harmony, and many owners of my puppies send or e-mail me photographs of their dogs and cats happily sleeping together. Many years ago I had a litter of 14 puppies and a young kitten I had at the time used to lie with them and play with them until of course, they as a group, became a bit too big and boisterous. However, she continued to be fascinated by them until they left for their new homes. The puppy we kept from that litter always loved the cat and often slept with her until he died of old age.

If people keep chickens or rabbits or guinea pigs in runs in the garden, the Border Collie will run round and round the enclosure or lie as if penning sheep. Be careful if the other pets are accustomed to running free, as most Border Collies will chase and perhaps kill what they see as food. I recently sold a year old dog to a family who owned a guinea pig called 'Galaxy'. We were all rather concerned for Galaxy's safety as he was accustomed to running freely about the garden and coming into the house. Fortunately the family were very sensible and they supervised introductions slowly and carefully over a period of time, with a successful result. I regularly receive pictures of 'Joe' the dog lying down, with his nose just touching Galaxy.

If mutual respect is established, the Border Collie will be an ideal family companion.

BORDER COLLIES AND CHILDREN

Puppies and children must be encouraged to respect one another and understand each other's needs. For the puppy, undisturbed rest is essential, as well as play, while he must be taught not to jump up or play bite fingers and toes.

If play biting occurs, a firm "No" or loud "Ouch" followed by ignoring the puppy is the way to curb this behaviour. The loud exclamation resembles the response of other littermates when biting is too much.

If the puppy jumps up at a child, a loud "Get off" followed by walking forward into the puppy is required, rather than backing off with hands in the air which merely encourages more jumping.

Having given these warnings,

children and dogs form strong bonds which often compensate for difficult periods in a child's life when adult human relationships become fraught.

TOWN OR COUNTRY?

Ideally Border Collies need space to run and this can be either open fields in the country or a park in a town. I walk my dogs at least three times a day and give them free running in a field. The most essential thing for a Border Collie is a fenced garden where he can roam freely and safely. A dry kennel with an open air run is better for a Border Collie than being left in the house while the owners are at work.

A flat or garden-less home is not a good place for a Border Collie as the restrictions can frustrate and wind up the dog.

Border Collies are active, intelligent dogs and should not be left all day in a crate whilst the owners are at work. Any breed of dog can become aggressive if it is left without exercise all day. Border Collies are built for running, and run they must.

SPECIAL SKILLS

The Border Collie is a highly intelligent breed and this intelligence, plus the Collie's huge desire to work, has been channelled into a number of specialist areas.

SEARCH AND RESCUE

The Border Collie is invaluable as a sniffer dog and for search and rescue. Initially the Border Collie was bred to search out lost lambs and sheep and to use his nose and inquisitiveness to do this job. This ability can be channelled

The Border Collie likes to use his initiative and makes a top-class search dog.

The breed is used successfully as a guide dog.

The Border Collie is a good choice for a therapy dog as he has a knack of tuning into people's feelings.

into searching for drugs, explosives and even lost bodies for the Police, Customs and Armed Forces. Border Collies were used in the Falklands War and in the recent Tsunami disaster.

Maggie Peacock and her Arnpriors Border Collies are specialists in this area of work and in Hungary Gábor Szábo is famous for his training of Border Collies in search and rescue.

ASSISTANCE DOGS

Border Collies have been used for many years as guide dogs for the blind. Their loyalty and will to please make them particularly suitable for this job. Alison Hornsby and her husband Leo have bred and trained many wonderful dogs for this purpose with the Bekkis affix.

DOGS FOR THE DISABLED

Border Collies can be trained to assist disabled people by bringing a cordless telephone to their owners, switching lights on and off and opening and closing doors. They will also pick up dropped items, put washing in the washing machine and a host of other useful tasks. Their adoring and faithful natures give emotional support as well as practical assistance and they are often the closest and sometimes the only friend of a disabled person living alone.

I had a friend who lived on a small farm. Her elderly mother lived in the annexe and was fiercely independent. The old lady owned a dog that died of old age and she was bereft. My friend asked me if I had an older dog who would be a companion for her mother. I gave her Jaffa, who was a sweet, loving bitch and content to lie around and go for occasional gentle walks. These two old ladies (the dog and her mistress) lived together until the end of their lives and were besotted with each other. You could see them regularly gazing into each other's eyes with complete adoration. When the old lady died Jaffa followed soon after. Border Collies can also detect auras and warn people who are about to have an epileptic fit. This enables the person to prepare themselves and so avoid injury.

THERAPY DOGS
Pets As Therapy or PAT dogs are highly regarded and valued. Border Collies are particularly good at visiting people in homes or hospitals.

I used to visit a 20-year-old girl with severe M.E. She needed

Once you have chosen a Border Collie, you will be hooked for life.

nurses to come each day to feed her and to turn her to prevent bedsores. I was told that she loved dogs and in fact, she had pictures of dogs all around her room.

I decided to take an eight week old puppy that I was running on from a litter. The puppy would just sit on my lap as I talked with the girl. Gradually she started to move her hand towards the puppy to stroke it. Eventually after a few visits, she was extending her whole arm and was obviously delighted by the presence and the feel of the soft fur of the puppy.

I was asked recently to go and give a talk on judging at Crufts to a group of elderly people, some of whom were very disabled. I took a 12 week old puppy to demonstrate the points

I was talking about. It soon became obvious which of the people had owned dogs or were interested in them. Some of the people wanted to stroke or cuddle the puppy, whilst others really came to life telling me about their pets and farm animals, as this was a rural area.

SUMMING UP
The Border Collie is one of the most versatile stars of the canine world. This multi-talented breed can thrive in many different roles, both as a working dog and as a pet. A high-energy, intelligent dog, the Border Collie is not for every would-be dog owner, but matched to the right home, able to fulfil his significant potential, this is a dog that will earn a special place in your heart.

THE FIRST BORDER COLLIES

Chapter 2

The Border Collie is a uniquely intelligent, energetic, loyal breed of herding dog with an fascinating history. Its development over the last 100 years emphasises the skill of breeding for the desired qualities, the versatility of this wonderful breed and the relationship between man and dog, both highly dependent on the other.

The Border country between England and Scotland over a century ago is the scene for the emergence of today's Border Collie. This had a thriving local woollen trade, depending on the sheep grazing on the Cheviot Hills in Northumbria and the Scottish Border region near its main river, the Tweed. The wool industry was then, as it is now, extremely important to the economy of the Borders, with world-renowned woollen mills in several Border towns such as Hawick, Selkirk and Galashiels. The local breed of sheep, the Cheviot, provided the durable wool which became

Andrew Brown's Old Maid.
© *International Sheep Dog Society, courtesy of Andrew Hall, Working Sheepdog Archive.*

famous as the tweed cloth produced in these Border mills. The importance therefore, of the shepherd and his dogs in this countryside, was as a corner stone to this industry. With the industrial revolution leading to highly mechanised mills, increased wool production and larger flocks of sheep, the shepherds looked to breed a more effective herding dog which was intelligent, biddable and with an instinctive desire to work closely with his handler.

Known as a 'working collie' in those days, the dog was bred primarily to herd sheep or cattle. There was some cross-breeding with other good working dogs, such as Bearded Collies and drovers' dogs, but the black, rough-coated dog with white on his collar, chest and tip of the tail was described over 200 years ago by Northumbrian naturalist Thomas Bewick in his book *The General History of Quadrupeds*, published in 1790. Around the same time in Scotland, the national bard Robert Burns described the black sheepdog with classic markings in his epic poem *The Twa Dogs*. One of the many verses describes the sheepdog named 'Luath' in these words:

Adam Telfer's Old Hemp. © *International Sheep Dog Society, courtesy of Andrew Hall, Working Sheepdog Archive.*

> *He was a gash and faithfu' tyke*
> (gash = wise)
> *As ever lap a sheuch or dyke*
> (sheuch = ditch)
> *His honest sonsie baws'nt face*
> (baws'nt = white striped)
> *Ay gat him friends in ilka place*
> (ilka = every)
> *His breast was white, his tousie back*
> (tousie = shaggy)
> *Weel clad wi' coat o' glossy black*
> *His gawsie tail wi' upward curl*
> (gawsie = handsome)
> *Hung ower his hurdies wi' a swirl.*
> (hurdies = hips)

CREATING A BREED

In the 19th century, many of these working collies were hard dogs, strong willed and rather aggressive with the sheep. But because of their strong eye and herding instincts, it seemed worth trying to cross them with a more biddable and obedient type of working collie. The shepherd who achieved this aim in a uniquely successful way was Adam Telfer, a Northumbrian with great expertise in breeding, training and handling these dogs. He succeeded in producing the right combination of qualities in his breeding lines. He used Roy as the sire, who was a good tempered, tri coloured dog – a good worker but without much eye – and put him to a very black bitch called Meg, who had different but complimentary working qualities. She was strong eyed but not very friendly. The resulting offspring included Hemp, born in 1893, who sired more than 200 puppies and is now widely acknowledged as being the founding father of the Border Collie.

Hemp was an exceptional worker with such strong herding instincts that he needed little training, and his temperament and personality were greatly admired. Virtually all Border Collies around the world today descend from Hemp, or Old Hemp as he is usually known. Shepherds around the country wanted to buy offspring or breed from these Border dogs because they recognised their excellent qualities. Telfer produced dogs which were properly built to do a day's work; they had stamina and power, yet an economy of movement which is a key characteristic of the Border Collie. They had a strong eye to control the sheep, yet a willingness to respond to their master's commands.

Today's Border Collies and their owners owe a great debt to the Telfer family. Adam's father Walter won the first sheepdog trial in England in 1876. Adam himself was born in 1859, and moved around various farms in Northumbria near the Cheviots. His sheepdogs were always part of the family. He knew that a working dog deserved good food, warm housing and yet would lose nothing in discipline. The dogs more than repaid his dedication and skills as a trainer. Adam and two of his sons, Walter and Adam Jnr. had great success on the trials field and in 1924 Adam Snr. won the English National Championship, Walter was second, and Adam Jnr. was well placed, so all three represented England at the International Championship that year. Adam Telfer Snr. was a great friend of William Wallace of Otterburn, the noted handler who introduced the 'silent' method of working dogs. Prior to that time shepherds and triallists had controlled their dogs by shouting, stamping and waving their crooks. William Wallace demonstrated that it was possible to quietly control a dog with low whistles and hisses.

GOING INTERNATIONAL

The International Sheep Dog Society (ISDS) was formed in 1906. At first the committee was composed solely of Scottish shepherds and farmers from the Borders. They organised a sheepdog trial at Gullane near Edinburgh, which attracted handlers from across the border in England and therefore was deemed to be 'international'. So, the International Sheepdog Trials were established and over the

Loos II, one of William Wallace's 'silent workers'.
© *International Sheep Dog Society, courtesy of Andrew Hall, Working Sheepdog Archive.*

years came to embrace Wales and Ireland. In 1915 James Reid became the Secretary of the ISDS and he is credited with coining the term 'Border Collie' in the papers he wrote on early working dogs. He began the record of Border Collies, which is the ISDS Stud Book. The first volume was printed 1955, but included dogs like Old Hemp who was given the number 9. Andrew Brown's bitch Old Maid has the honour of being number 1.

The ISDS Stud Book enables the lines from Old Hemp to be traced to some very influential dogs, such as his grandson Isaac Herdman's Tommy 16 (Number 16 in the ISDS Stud Book). He was bred by William Wallace, the great sheepdog breeder and handler. Tommy had considerable

success at trials and was used extensively at stud. Mated to G.P Brown's Nell 205, he produced an amazing line of International Champions, including G. P Brown's Spot 308.

When researching the overseas connections, we can see that some very prominent people emerge. In New Zealand, in the early 1900s, James Lilico imported many excellent Border Collies from contacts he had in the Border region. Originally a shepherd in County Antrim in Ireland, he emigrated to New Zealand in 1894. A bitch called Hindhope Jed was sent from Scotland first to James Lilico in New Zealand, and was then bought in 1901 by Alec McLeod for the princely sum of £25 whilst on a visit from New South Wales, Australia. Jed is acknowledged to be the first Border Collie in Australia and had great success at trials, winning the 1903 Sydney Sheep Show Trial. The reputation of these early dogs spread and led to a real demand for other imports from Britain, including the 1907 Supreme Champion William Wallace's Moss 22, renamed Border Boss after arriving in New Zealand. His sire was the famous Isaac Herdman's Tommy 16.

In the USA Sam Stoddart imported not only Supreme Champion Spot 308, but many other top trial dogs which had a huge influence on the bloodlines

SPOT ON

Spot 308 became a key dog not only in Britain but also in the United States of America and Australia. George P. Brown, his owner, was the youngest of three Scottish brothers who farmed in Berwickshire around the time of the First World War. Spot 308 was born in 1920 and was successful in trials at an early age. He was a handsome black and white dog with spotted legs and semi erect ears. He had a kindly temperament with adults and children, and was trained by George P. Brown, who put all his young dogs on ducks before letting them work with sheep.

In 1923 Spot 308 won the Scottish National and then the Supreme International Championship. He was only three years old at that time and had not yet been used at stud. That same year he was sold and exported to Mr Sam Stoddart in the USA where he had a very significant influence on bloodlines in North America. Before he left the UK however, he was mated to some 25 bitches and produced exceptional progeny, including the successful trialist Moss 454, owned by C.B. MacPherson. Moss in turn was sent on the long sea journey to Australia to James Moore in Victoria, where he helped found the Boveagh and Kyneton kennels and had a very significant influence on the breeding lines in Australia and New Zealand. Chris Howe of the Kyneton kennels in Victoria wrote that McPherson's Moss 454 was "the greatest sire ever seen in the Southern hemisphere".

Spot 308
*Photo from the Barbara
Carpenter collection,
courtesy of Andrew Hall,
Working Sheepdog Archive.*

**JM Wilson with
four of his dogs.**

*Photo from the John
Herries McCulloch
'Border Collie Studies'
collection, courtesy of
Andrew Hall, Working
Sheepdog Archive.*

in North America. Stoddart was a Scot who also had strong connections to the Borders region.

In the 1930s, the name of J.M. Wilson stands out as the most successful sheepdog handler and possibly the greatest ever. J.M. Wilson won eleven National and nine International Championships – the first in 1928 with Fly 824 and the last in 1950 with Mirk 4438. Fly was seven generations from Old Hemp. Four generations take us back to Herdman's Tommy 16, and a further three from Tommy to Old Hemp. Some 20 years later, Mirk was a total of 12 generations from Old Hemp. Mirk's pedigree highlights the

importance of another very significant dog with a great influence on today's Border Collie. This dog is Mirk's grandsire J.M. Wilson's Cap 3036.

OUTSTANDING INFLUENCES

There are few of today's dogs who do not have Cap 3036 in their bloodlines He was bred in 1937 by Hugh Cullens in Perthshire, a breeder with great skill in producing excellent working dogs. J.M. Wilson eventually bought Cap when he was around two years old. At that time he lived at Whitehope, Innerleithen in the Scottish Borders, the home of many

illustrious Border Collies. Cap 3036 was a big black and white rough coated dog with a good deal of white marking on him. One side of his head was white with a black ear, the other side black. He had a wonderful temperament and was a very willing worker. The major sheepdog trials were cancelled during the Second World War from 1939 until 1945, so Cap was unable to demonstrate his skills on the trials field. His reputation however, spread extensively and he sired hundreds of puppies of which 188 were registered, including 112 bitches.

Stories of Cap 3036 include one where two shepherds and

their dogs were unable to gather 200 to 300 sheep on the hills near Peebles in bad weather. They returned home defeated, so J.M. Wilson set out on horseback alone with Cap to try again. A short time later J.M. Wilson returned, followed by the sheep safely driven home under Cap's sole command.

Cap 3036 is line bred back to another very significant dog Hemp 153, bred by Adam Telfer and owned by Tom Dickson. Hemp was an excellent worker and enjoyed travelling to trials in Mr. Dickson's motorcycle sidecar. Examining the pedigree of Cap 3036, it is clear that Dickson's Hemp 153 is four generations back on both the sire and dam's sides and another six generations takes us back to Old Hemp. The list of winning dogs descending from Cap 3036 is endless, including many great champions such as the Supreme Champions of 1950 and 1951 respectively, Mirk 4438 and Pat 4203. In both cases Cap 3036 was their maternal grandsire.

The influence of Cap 3036 was emphasised in the 1960s when Wiston Cap 31154 appeared on the trials scene. At the tender age of 21 months he won the Supreme Championship in 1965 for his trainer and handler John Richardson of Peebles. Wiston Cap was line bred by W.S. Hetherington with Cap 3036 appearing sixteen times within seven generations, so it is no

Cap 3036. *Photo from the John Herries McCulloch 'Border Collie Studies' collection, courtesy of Andrew Hall, Working Sheepdog Archive.*

surprise that he inherited so many of his ancestor's qualities as a working dog and, like Cap 3036, he also had a half white face.

Wiston Cap sired three Supreme Champions: Bill 51654, Cap 50543 and Glen 47241, and is grandsire to three others: Bess 101142, Bill 78263 and Mirk 67512. Some of his descendants were exported to the USA. His grandson Bill 102167 won the North American Championship while Bill's brother Sweep 102166 was Kentucky Blue Grass Champion.

Wiston Cap proved to be a very popular sire, possibly the most widely used stud dog in the breed of all time. His offspring tended to inherit his biddable nature and his ability to work with the minimum of commands, particularly on the outfield. Cap was such a quick learner that John Richardson used to lie awake at night thinking up

something new to teach him in the morning. They made a wonderful partnership and crowds came from far and near to watch them at trials or giving demonstrations. Wiston Cap lived to the ripe old age of 15 and a half years and his passing was mourned by the sheepdog world, none more so than his master. His name is legendary in the world of Border Collies. His characteristic crouching pose has become world famous as the logo for the ISDS and his name will always be remembered with pride.

THE FIGHT FOR RECOGNITION

As well as being a first-class working dog, the Border Collie is beautifully built and a joy to watch on the move. So the desire grew that perhaps they could become masters of the show ring. Proud shepherds and trialists often enjoyed the extra interest of a 'beauty competition' held after various trials. In fact at the very first sheepdog trial in Wales held at Bala, a dog called Tweed won not only the trial, but was selected as the most handsome dog. Of course we cannot guess what the criteria were, but it is quite something to come off a trial field in a handsome state. Careful breeding and the meticulous records kept by the ISDS should have created the perfect scenario for the Border Collie to gain early

THE VERSATILE BORDER COLLIE

During the 1960s and 1970s, there was growing interest in the sports of obedience and agility along with working trials. The early clubs were often founded by police dog handlers, wishing to hone their skills and give their dogs an extra outlet for their energies. These were German Shepherd Dogs, or Alsatians as they were commonly known in those days. The clubs encouraged non-police personnel to become more involved in having well trained dogs. Many of the people who are significant in the world of obedience today started out by owning and training German Shepherds to a high standard, but then Border Collies began to take part and they very soon began to outclass the GSDs. At first these Border Collies were either unregistered farm dogs, or they were carefully selected from ISDS lines, with a keenness to work coupled with trainability and the personality required in a family dog.

The Crufts Obedience Champion of 1958/62/64 and 1966 was Muriel Pearce's Megan of Monksmead who carries Cap 3036 four times in five generations. She also has behind her the 1947 Supreme Champion Spot 3624 and 1950 Supreme Champion Mirk 4438, plus several other excellent trial dogs. Megan only had one successful mating and that was to Obedience Champion Patanne 14511. Of the six pups, three became Obedience Champions.

By now Border Collies were being bred specifically to compete in obedience competitions and other sports, always with a view to keeping the breed's strong working instinct and yet making these dogs suitable as family pets if in the right hands. Although many of these dogs descended from Wiston Cap, there were some breeders like Bing Bellamy of the Sealight kennels and Eileen Stone of the Gemond kennels, who with one exception, chose completely different lines so that outcrossing was always an option. The Sealight Border Collies descended from Patanne and Megan, along with Supreme Champion Garry 17690 and Supreme Champion Glen 3940. The Gemond lines also included Garry 17690 along with Supreme Champion Ken 17166 and Scottish National Champion Spot 24981. You will find the name Gemond behind many of today's Border Collies still involved in sports and in the show ring as ancestors of the Detania and Caristan lines for example. The Sealights too have made their mark and appear in pedigrees of Mobella, Sheltysham and Tidespring in the UK plus the Greatglen dogs which were exported to the USA in the 1990s.

When you consider that the Border Collie only evolved as a pure breed at the turn of the 20th century, it has made enormous strides in the affection of the British people. Initially they were seen as being solely useful working dogs but gradually they began to excel at almost every task they were given.

Jock Richardson with his three Champion dogs – Sweep, Wiston Cap and Mirk.

© International Sheep Dog Society, courtesy of Andrew Hall, Working Sheepdog Archive.

Kennel Club recognition as a pedigree breed, but it was felt that there still was not enough regularity of 'type'. The Kennel Club was however, happy to put Border Collies on their 'Activity Register' for the increasing numbers of the breed who were successfully involved in obedience.

By the early 1960s there was a groundswell of enthusiasm among obedience people that the Kennel Club should give the breed pedigree status. The ISDS was originally reluctant, believing that the working ability of the Border Collie would be compromised, and it was not until 1976 that the Kennel Club in conjunction with the ISDS announced that the

Border Collie would be recognised as a breed for show purposes. For several years some Border Collie breeders continued to register pups with both organisations, but now dual registration is becoming rarer. On average the ISDS registers 6,000 dogs annually, whereas the Kennel Club in recent years has an annual total of around 2,200, which includes new puppies, the Activity Register and importations.

The Border Collie Club of Great Britain was founded in 1973 and became a vital voice for Border Collie enthusiasts. One of the early difficulties in showing and judging the breed at Kennel Club events, was that there was no Breed Standard. This is the blueprint which describes how a

particular breed of dog should look: how tall should he be?; what colours are permissible?; what length should the muzzle be?; how should the dog move? The answer lay across the world in Australia, where Border Collies had been exhibited since 1907. Standards were drawn up in Queensland and New South Wales after the Second World War and a national Standard was adopted and approved by the Australian National Kennel Council in 1963.

A few alterations had to be made to meet UK needs; for example, prick-eared dogs may be shown in the UK but not in Australia. With the prick-eared Wiston Cap behind so many British dogs, they are bound to pop up in the breed and are certainly popular with shepherds. An interim Standard was accepted by the Kennel Club in 1979 and two years later it was announced that the breed's first Challenge Certificates would be awarded at Crufts 1982. There was a huge buzz of excitement when the day arrived. Which dog and bitch would the judge Catherine Sutton choose to be the UK's first C.C. winners?

The dog Challenge Certificate went to Tilehouse Cassius of Beagold, a black and white dog bred by Iris Combe by her Brocken Sweep of Tilehouse 96909 out of Fly of Tilehouse 89880 and owned by Joyce Collis and Felix Cosme. The first Crufts bitch C.C. went to Tracelyn Gal owned and handled by Eric Broadhurst. She was by Welsh

National Champion Cymro 82447 out of J.E. Ritchie's Jill 89227 and was black, white and tan. 'Emma', as she was known, was also a TV star in *Sherlock Holmes* and in the long running soap opera *Coronation Street*.

The two major types of show in the UK are Championship shows where Challenge Certificates are on offer to the breed and Open shows without CCs. In general, Championship shows attract Border Collie entries of between 150 and 200. At Crufts the entry is nearer 400 and requires a judge for each sex. The various Border Collie clubs around the country hold both Championship and Open shows, which generally are very well supported. On a local level there are Open shows catering for a variety of breeds and Border Collies are usually included. An entry of 20 to 30 is respectable. Points can be collected at both Open and Championship shows towards the title Junior Warrant and at Open shows towards the Show Certificate of Merit.

A Border Collie dog or bitch who gains three Challenge Certificates under different judges, is given the title Show Champion. The UK's first Show Champions were Tilehouse Cassius of Beagold

Sh. Ch. Muirend Border Dream: One of the breed's first Show Champions.

and Nan Simpson's beautiful homebred Muirend Border Dream. She was by Pioneer of Muirend out of Nimble of Muirend and her pedigree includes several eminent working dogs, including the 1975 Scottish National Champion Mirk 52844. Like Cassius, she descends from Old Hemp through Brown's Spot 308.

It was agreed with the ISDS that the full title of Champion could only be given to those dogs that also passed a complex sheep herding test devised by the ISDS and judged by two of their representatives. A dog was only entitled to take the test if it had already qualified for a Kennel Club Stud Book number, by being very highly placed at Championship shows, being a Junior Warrant holder or having a top placing at ISDS sheepdog trials. Already a

difficult test, it was amended in 1992 and became a rigorous challenge even for dogs accustomed to working sheep. It comprised an outrun of 200 yards, a lift, fetch and drive of 100 yards and herding ten sheep into a twelve foot pen within 12 minutes. The test could only be taken three times, twice in any given year. It is therefore hardly surprising that few people in the show fraternity even attempted the test. Also they were reluctant to introduce their dogs to sheep work that they might not be able to continue. The first few dogs to pass the test all had experience of running in sheepdog trials.

One of the dogs to pass the test in 1994 was Heather Turner's homebred four year old Locheil Look North (Nap). The winner of two Challenge Certificates, Nap's parentage was top drawer being by Show Champion Viber Travelling Matt from Corinlea JW, winner of 30 Challenge Certificates, out of Lethans Jace, a beautiful bitch. Nap gained his third Challenge Certificate the following year, thus becoming the breed's first and so far only Champion. The Border Collie clubs and the breed council have recently been working alongside the ISDS and Kennel Club to make the working test more

Sh.Ch. Viber Travelling Matt from Corinlea JW: Winner of 30 Challenge Certificates.

Whenway Mist of Wizaland: An Obedience Champion and a Show Champion.

realistic and more appealing to the owners of show dogs.

Another singular achievement was realised by Sue Large, when her Whenway Mist of Wizaland became first an Obedience Champion in 1984 and then a Show Champion in 1989. Mist was a very intelligent bitch with a strong sense of fun. She and Sue made a wonderful team.

NEW ZEALAND IMPORTS
The year 1989 was highly significant for show Border Collies in the UK, when Sue Large imported Francesca of Clan-Abby from Judy Vos in New Zealand. Francesca, a New Zealand Champion, was in whelp to NZ Champion Clan-Abby Casanova Too and the resulting litter was so exceptional that Sue wanted to keep all of the pups, but Pam Harris of Mobella persuaded her to part with Wizaland Newz Speculation. In due time these pups produced

some wonderful offspring for a wide number of British kennels. At the same time, Bruce and Sheena Kilsby of Whenway brought over NZ Champion Clan-Abby Blue Aberdoone, who became a British Show Champion in 1990 and began to make his mark as a stud dog.

There was, however, some resistance to these new imports, particularly the feeling that British Border Collies would become simply pretty creatures and would lose their brains and herding ability. In fact, Blue was descended from many significant British working dogs which had been sent to New Zealand many years before and traces back to Old Hemp in 20 generations; eight generations to Australian Champion Clivus Cloud, seven more to Supreme Champion Spot 308 and then a further five to Old Hemp. Blue certainly exhibited herding instincts which he was able to pass on. One of

his daughters Ma Biche of Whenway was so successful at sheepdog trials that she was registered on merit by the ISDS. Blue Aberdoone became a UK Show Champion within a few months of his arrival and was Best of Breed at Crufts in 1991. One of his sons, Show Champion Clan-Abby Silver Kiwi at Beagold, was Crufts Best of Breed in 1993.

When Blue was mated to Altricia Pandora at Dykebar, a star was born in the form of the aptly named Dykebar Future Glory (Sky), who was bred and owned by John and Lorraine Ritchie. She was beautifully constructed and simply flowed round the show ring, enjoying every moment. Sky had enormous success, becoming the breed's female record holder with 39 Challenge Certificates; her finest hour was winning Reserve Best in Show at Crufts 1994. What an achievement for a breed which had been allocated its first CCs only 12 years before.

NZ Ch. Clan-Abby Blue Aberdoone: A highly influential stud dog.

Grand Ch. Am. Ch. Nahrof First Edition CD.

Irish Ch. Tonkory Move Over to Huntly, (co-owned by David and Morag Connolly and Judith Gregory) the only Border Collie pup to go Best in Show at a UK All-Breed Championship Show at seven and a half months.

Grand Ch. Borderfame Heart N' Soul.

Show Champion Clan-Abby Blue Aberdoone's influence can be seen in the quality of progeny produced in many British kennels even after four generations, when carefully blended with other lines. Among his descendants is the current UK record holder with 45 Challenge Certificates, Show Champion Tonkory Palmerston at Fayken JW who was bred by Judith Gregory and is owned by Ross and Vicki Green.

THE AMERICAN BORDER COLLIE

In the USA the breed was recognised by the American Kennel Club in 1995, despite opposition from organisations representing sheepdog trials. It was virtually impossible to build up a show kennel from American working lines and so Border Collies were imported from the UK and then increasingly from New Zealand and Australia. The early winners represented that trend. The first breed Champion was New Zealand Champion Clan-Abby to Hell and Back, owned by the Darkwind kennels and the first male champion was Kiwi Envoy from Clan-Abby, owned by Debbie Wood. The accolade of being the first Best in Show Border Collie at an all breeds championship show in the USA, came to Australian Champion Nahrof First Edition, bred in Australia by Lauren Somers and Errol Badoir. He was a very handsome, eye catching dog with a wonderful temperament. All of these winners descend from Old Hemp through Moss 454 and his influence on the Kyneton kennels. The breed continues to grow in popularity in America, enjoying many activities including a herding test. In 2006 there were 2181 Border Collie pups registered in the USA.

GRAND CHAMPION

British breeders continue to occasionally import stock from overseas and in 2000 a very special dog arrived on our shores.

He was Australian Grand Champion Borderfame Heart N Soul, otherwise known as Denver. He was bred by Helena Fitzgerald and spent some time in the USA, becoming an American Champion. While resident in Europe he collected the titles Luxemburg, Dutch and Polish Champion, and then he came to the UK to live with Judith Gregory of Tonkory Kennels. He quickly added Show Champion to his titles and won the Dog Challenge Certificate at Crufts in 2002 and 2003. Returning to Helena he was Top Show Dog All Breeds for Western Australia for three consecutive years. When used at stud he produced outstanding progeny for many kennels worldwide, including several Show Champions, plus CC and Reserve CC winners. Denver also descends from the old British Border Collies through Kyneton Moss, a son of Moss 454 and several other lines.

BRITISH INFLUENCE

It is worth noting that not all top winning dogs in the UK descend from imported bloodlines. In 2005 and 2006 four new Show Champions carried only British lines. These were:

- Sheltysham Shay of Corinlea, who descends from Show Champion Viber Travelling Matt from Corinlea and Show Champion Tilehouse Cassius of Beagold.
- Grandver Celtic Quest, who also descends from the above dogs plus the famous Show

Champion Melodor Flint at Dykebar, who has Muirend ancestors including the half brother of the first female Show Champion.

- Altricia Cali-fornia, whose lines also include Melodor Flint plus Show Champion Fieldbank Professional, who is line bred from Megan of Monksmead
- Tonkory Sanna at Corinlea, whose paternal grandsire is the breed's only full Champion, Locheil Look North.

Of course they all descend from Old Hemp.

CENTENARY CELEBRATIONS

As the ISDS was founded in 1906, it was appropriate that their Centenary International Supreme Championship should return to the Scottish Borders in 2006. The trial was held near Duns in Berwickshire on an undulating course in very miserable weather, but the usual camaraderie prevailed. It was good to see that some people from the show fraternity had come along to cheer on their favourites and see how Old Hemp's other descendents had evolved. It is always heartening to find so many similarities. The International Supreme Champion

Bobby Dalziel with International Supreme Champion Joe.
Photo © Austin Bennett, courtesy of Austin Bennett and Andrew Hall, Working Sheepdog Archive.

was Joe 272330, owned and handled by Bobby Dalziel from the Scottish Borders. Joe descends from many National and Supreme Champions including the great Wiston Cap 31154 and thus to all of the wonderful early dogs from which the Border Collie evolved.

As the spectators travelled home through the Border lands, did they pause for a moment to watch on the hillside some humble sheepdogs going about their daily work with effortless grace, intelligence and joy? They too have the blood of Telfer's Old Hemp coursing in their veins. We have inherited a wonderful legacy in these remarkable dogs.

A BORDER COLLIE FOR YOUR LIFESTYLE

3 Chapter

Buying a Border Collie puppy or taking on an older Border Collie needs a great deal of careful thought. It is a huge commitment that will affect your life for many years.

Your Border Collie will need attention and affection every day, so you have to consider whether you will have enough time to devote to him. No dog should be left for longer than four hours a day and in the case of a small puppy, for considerably less. In no circumstances should a Border Collie be left for a whole day while the family is at work; not only would this be grossly unfair on the dog, it is also inviting major behavioural problems.

Border Collies get bored very quickly when left alone and they may end up being destructive or making enough noise to cause complaints from the neighbours.

If you are likely to be away from home for more than a few hours, you will need to arrange for someone to walk your Border Collie for you, or at the very least, let him out in the garden and spend some time with him. If this is a rare occurrence, you may be able to arrange for a friend or neighbour to look after your Border Collie for a few hours. But if it is routine and regular, i.e. for the whole working day of each week, then you may have to consider hiring the services of a professional dog walker.

There are other costs you will need to be aware of. Veterinary fees, for example, can be very expensive. Can you afford the cost of veterinary insurance or vets' bills? Even the routine costs of vaccinations, worming tablets and eye and ear drops need to be taken into account, as Border Collies can be affected by a range

of minor ailments. You may wish to restrict your holidays to those which can include your dog, otherwise the cost of boarding your Border Collie in kennels or having someone in to house-sit while you are away, is also an expense that you will have to think about. It is only sensible to give careful thought to all the financial repercussions of owning a Border Collie before purchasing a puppy or an adult dog.

CAN YOU KEEP UP?

Border Collies are not couch potatoes; they are a very active breed and need regular daily exercise whatever the weather. Some time will also need to be spent training them (see Chapter 6: Training and Socialisation). If you have a Border Collie puppy, you will need to find a puppy socialising group and a good training class. It cannot be emphasised enough, how very

You need to commit the time to socialising your Border Collie as he is growing up.

important it is to take the time and effort to train your puppy or adult dog properly. The time and effort put into training and socialising a puppy will, however, be well rewarded. Behavioural problems with older Border Collies are nearly always caused by the lack of time and effort put into training the puppy in his early days.

When it comes to exercise, it is important to ensure that your puppy does not overdo it. You will need to restrict him until his bones and joints are fully developed to avoid straining and possible damage. For a Border Collie puppy, this time of rapid development of bones and joints should be complete at about a year old and the exercise regime

can be changed to that of a young vigorous adult dog.

However, once he is full grown there is nothing a Border Collie likes better than a l-o-n-g walk. Remember, he was originally bred to keep going all day long as a working sheepdog, so a quick trot around the block is decidedly not what he will have in mind!

WHAT DOG?

Is a Border Collie really the right breed for you? If you are looking for a dog for working or sports such as Obedience, Agility or Flyball, then the Border Collie should be high on your list of suitable breeds. If on the other hand, you want a Border Collie as a pet or companion, there are a range of households for which a

vigorous, bursting-with-energy dog such as a Border Collie, may not be a suitable choice. It may not for example, be the right breed for a retired couple, nor for a family with very small children.

If you have toddlers, will they be able to cope with a very boisterous puppy nibbling at their fingers and toes and running off with their toys? Will you be able to cope with a puppy and small children, especially when the weather is bad and they all have to be indoors most of the day? If you have a young family and you are thinking of taking on an older Border Collie, you need to be sure that he is used to children. Some Border Collies can be worried by childrens' quick movements and high-pitched voices. Careful supervision will be needed to avoid conflict or problems.

If you want to buy a Kennel Club or International Sheep Dog Society (ISDS) registered Border Collie, responsible breeders will first ask what you want him for – showing, working, sports (Obedience, Agility or Flyball), or pet – as well as whether you want a male or female and/or a particular colour. Before you talk to the breeder, you should be fairly certain in your own mind what you want, so that the breeder can concentrate on the attributes that suit your requirements.

Whatever your choice, character and temperament are things you should value most. There is no doubt that owning a Border Collie opens up a wide and exciting range of opportunities to compete with your dog, though you have to be prepared to work hard. Many people will have seen the wonderful television series *One Man And His Dog* and watched the marvellous interaction and co-ordination between the handler and his Border Collie. It doesn't happen by chance. In order to work sheep, the Border Collies will have received countless hours of intensive training, while most competitors will have worked sheep for many years on their farms.

You may have seen Obedience, Agility and Flyball competitions at Crufts on television. Many of the dogs competing are Border Collies. Doubtless you admired

If you want to compete in one of the canine sports, such as agility, a Border Collie is a natural choice.

the absolute precision of Obedience and the quick-mindedness, accuracy and speed of Agility and Flyball. For many people, the high spot of Crufts is the grace and precision of Mary Ray and her Border Collies demonstrating Heelwork to Music.

There are now many local and national clubs that specialise in Working Trials, Obedience, Agility, Flyball and Heelwork to Music and they organise and run various grades of competitions; some of which can eventually culminate in an appearance at Crufts. Quite often these clubs specialise in more than one of these disciplines.

There is more than one Border Collie show breeder who

originally bought their first Collie as a pet or for sporting competition and were then advised by others (not necessarily the breeder) to show their Border Collie in breed shows. Success often leads to a growing interest in showing and breeding Border Collies.

If you wish to show a Border Collie you will want one that has many of the attributes in the Breed Standard, which is a blueprint of what the perfect Border Collie should look like (See Chapter 7: The Perfect Border Collie). If you are a novice, you will need the advice of the breeder to help you choose the right puppy. You may also wish to seek the advice of other handlers and breeders who

You may have ambitions to get involved with showing your Border Collie.

You may decide upon the breeder of the style of Border Collie you like straightaway, but if not, you can select a shortlist of breeders that you might want to purchase from. You will be able to see the temperaments of the Border Collies both inside and outside the ring, so you can judge if they are friendly with people and other dogs. At the shows it may be possible to chat to breeders and handlers, but do not be upset if they do not have time to answer many questions. It can get very hectic at times if a breeder or handler is showing in more than one class. You can however, always ask for a contact phone number to enable you to talk to them at a later date. If you do see breeding that looks just right for you, it may well be that you will have to join a waiting list. Nevertheless, it is better to wait for what you really want rather than settle for second best.

If you are looking for a sports Border Collie then attend some of the various events. Talk to the owners and handlers of the Border Collies that catch your eye and ask who bred their dogs, but also watch the Border Collies when they are not working or competing and decide on the temperament you want to live with. Some sports dogs can be really 'full on' and never want to stop being on the go; others can be perfectly relaxed when they are not working.

If you are looking for a pet or companion Border Collie, it is probably best to go to the show lines as these lines tend to be

specialise in the breed.

To show a Border Collie (or any breed of dog for that matter) correctly, the main quality a handler must have is the ability to give the show judge every opportunity to see the best of the Border Collie's attributes against the Breed Standard. This requires some of the skills of obedience trainers.

FINDING A BREEDER

If you are choosing a puppy, you are about to embark on a relationship which will hopefully, last up to 15 years or more, so it is worth the time spent doing plenty of research in the first place. You need to decide what you want from your puppy or adult dog. Are you looking for a companion, a show dog, a working dog or a sports dog?

If you want to purchase a puppy to show, try to attend as many breed shows as possible, where you will be able to see lots of different types of Border Collie. You should make a point of finding out who the breeders are by purchasing a show catalogue which lists all the Border Collies and their owners and breeders.

If you want to compete with your dog, talk to a breeder who specialises in producing dogs for specific disciplines.

more laid back. This is not to say that the Border Collies bred from show lines cannot do all the activities, but usually they are less intense about it than some of the sports or working bred Border Collies.

CHOOSING A PUPPY

Once you are certain that a Border Collie is the right breed for you, you need to decide whether you would like a bitch or a dog. Bitches are a little smaller in size and therefore, not as strong physically, but you will have to consider how you will cope with your bitch coming into season. Even if you intend to have her spayed, it is best to wait until after she has had at least one season. Males are bigger and

stronger and are more likely to develop a tendency to wander, unless they are properly trained.

Border Collies come in a wide range of colours, so decide what colour you would like. Some of the more unusual colours, such as red merle, may be difficult to obtain and you may have to travel some distance to find a puppy. If you are hoping to show your puppy, an evenly marked puppy is best, whatever colour you choose.

Do not be surprised or offended if the breeder asks you many questions about yourself and your lifestyle, as any responsible breeder will want to make sure that you and the puppy are suited to each other. He or she may want to visit you

and your family in your own home and is certainly likely to want to maintain contact once you have your puppy.

Make sure that your puppy comes from parents who have been hip scored and have been DNA tested for the various hereditary diseases which can affect Border Collies, such as Trapped Neutrophil Syndrome (TNS), Collie Eye Anomaly (CEA), Progressive Retinal Atrophy (PRA) and Ceroid Lipofuscinosis (CL) (See Chapter 8: Happy and Healthy). All responsible breeders will have had these tests done, so you should ask to see the relevant paperwork and certificates, as well as the registrations.

You should also ask whether

Some of the more unusual colours, such as red merle, may take some tracking down.

the puppies have been reared in an outside kennel or in the house. In the case of the latter they will be used to general family life activities including the noises of the vacuum cleaner, washing machine and television. Crucially, they are also more likely to be used to people. As puppies grow however, they need fresh air, sunshine and space to run and play, so most good breeders will divide the puppies' time between being indoors and outside.

See as many of the puppy's relatives as possible. It is always an advantage to be able to see close relatives, as this can give you an idea of the kind of dog your puppy will grow up to be. It is seldom possible to see the sire of the litter, since the dam is likely to have been mated to a dog from another kennel. If the dam has had previous litters, ask if it is possible to see the offspring. Whatever happens, you *must* see the puppies with their

mother. It is important to know that she is friendly and outgoing in temperament.

Breeders vary as to when they will allow the puppies to be visited. Some welcome visitors while the puppies are still very young, although puppies cannot see or hear until they are two to three weeks old and if they are well looked after, sleep most of the time until they are about four weeks old. For that reason most breeders will recommend waiting

You will want to see the mother with her puppies as this will give you some idea of the temperament they are likely to inherit.

until the puppies are a few weeks old before you visit them.

Watch the puppies playing with their littermates, as this will give you an indication of their character and temperament. The livelier puppies may possibly be best for working, the quieter ones may be better as pets; however, that is a very rough guide, as their character may change once they are in their new home away from their littermates.

A good breeder will happily give you advice on which puppy he or she feels would be the best for you. They are with the litter all the time, so they really get to know each member of it. By the way, you should not pick up the puppies unless the breeder gives you permission.

Do not be tempted to choose a Border Collie puppy purely on its markings when it is tiny. Wait until the breeder can advise you

on the developing conformation, character and temperament of the puppy before you make your decision. In particular, if you are looking for a puppy to show, you will need to wait until the puppy is old enough for you and the breeder to assess its conformation.

WORKING LINES

All Border Collies retain working instincts, but obviously those that come directly from working lines rather than show lines are likely to have stronger instincts and may not make such good family pets. Choosing a dog that does not have a very strong work drive is the best way to be sure he will develop into a good family companion as his instincts can be diverted more easily into other forms of activities.

Be aware that within a single litter there will be different

personalities and pups with different talents. It is hard to be sure about what is inherited and what is learnt even in the very early days from the mother. But a pup is more likely to have a good temperament if his mother has a sound temperament. Pups also vary in their talents. For example, for scenting, hearing, in their physical stamina, whether they are busy or lazy, keen to work or not as keen to work and also whether they have a dominant or passive temperament.

Avoid buying unsocialised litters from farm gates. You may be lucky, but the chances are that you will get a dog with a very strong work instinct and he may think that in the absence of sheep that people are the animal to be 'worked'. (See Chapter Six Training and Socialisation). If, however, such a dog is given time, training and mental stimulation,

CHOOSING A PUPPY

How do you know
which puppy will suit
your lifestyle?

Watch the puppies play
together and you will see
their individual personalities
start to emerge.

If you are looking for a show puppy, the breeder will help you to assess conformation and markings.

There may be one puppy that seems to say "pick me"...

If you plan to rehome an older dog, try to find out as much as possible about his past history.

then the match can be very successful.

PAPERWORK

When you collect your puppy, you should be given a copy of his pedigree, his Kennel Club or ISDS registration papers and other relevant paperwork regarding health checks of both the parents and puppy. A responsible breeder will also give you an advice sheet on diet and details of the puppy's worming regime, plus free veterinary insurance cover for the first few weeks.

Ask the breeder if there is a local Border Collie breed club or dog training club which you can join. Whether you hope to show or work your Border Collie, or have him as a much loved family pet, a local breed or training club will be able to offer you advice and support. Most clubs organise a variety of different events in which you may enjoy taking part

and you will meet other Border Collie lovers, too.

CHOOSING AN ADULT

When it comes to choosing an adult Border Collie, always try and find out as much as possible about his background so that you know what you are dealing with. By doing so, you will make it much easier for the Border Collie to settle in to his new home.

Some breeders re-home young adult Border Collies from time to time. They may have had one returned to them as the result of a marriage break-up for example, so it is always worth contacting them to see if they have anything available themselves or know of someone else who has. There are many rescue societies, including some that deal only with Border Collies. A local breeder or breed club secretary would be able to put you in touch with the latter. Vets also sometimes know of

Border Collies needing new homes.

If you do want an older Border Collie, you will still be asked lots of questions about yourself, your lifestyle and your home and garden. The rescue society may even visit you in your own home. Do not take on an older Border Collie thinking this is the easy option as regards house training and training in general, as you will still have to be prepared to put in a great deal of work accustoming the Border Collie to your way of life.

When taking on an adult, you and the Border Collie will need time to bond, so be prepared to be very patient and do not expect too much too soon. At first, just spend time getting used to each other. Lots of praise and tasty treats will help the process. Once you and your Border Collie are happy and relaxed in each other's company, you can begin training

It is important that the whole family is involved in the decision to take on a Border Collie puppy.

together. Remember to take it slowly though, as your Border Collie may need to re-learn commands and how to respond to your way of training.

Be very careful about letting a newly acquired older Border Collie off the lead to begin with. Choose somewhere which is well fenced and use a long line or extendable lead until he responds immediately when you call him back. He has to get used to you and his new surroundings.

However, there is nothing more rewarding than seeing the relationship develop between a Border Collie and his new owner, once he has settled into his new way of life.

AND FINALLY

Make sure that when you first bring your Border Collie home, you have a couple of weeks at least with little happening in your household. This will give him plenty of time to settle in and become used to your routine. If you are aware that anything major is likely to change in the foreseeable future – for example the arrival of a new baby or an imminent holiday – it is best to wait until your life is more settled before introducing a dog.

The whole family needs to want to have a Border Collie, not just some of them, as he will change everyone's life once he

arrives. They will all have to remember to close doors and gates so that he doesn't escape and to put their clothes, shoes, toys and valuables out of reach, so that the dog does not chew them.

A Border Collie should never be purchased 'for the children'. He is not a toy to be discarded when the novelty wears off.

Border Collies require regular grooming. If you are houseproud, bear in mind that they usually have a thick undercoat, as well as a long topcoat. They shed hair most of the time and when they really moult, you will find dog hairs absolutely everywhere!

THE NEW ARRIVAL

4 Chapter

Preparation for bringing your new puppy or dog home should begin well in advance. Fences round the garden should be checked, making sure there are no gaps or holes through which a puppy can escape. Ensure that gates, especially wrought iron ones, don't have big gaps between the bars, as a puppy can wriggle through the tiniest of spaces. If you plan on getting an adult dog, ensure that the fences are high enough to stop him jumping out of your garden. Make sure that things like slug pellets, anti-freeze and any other toxic or poisonous substances are well out of reach and also that the bolts and catches on your garden sheds and garages are secure, so your puppy or dog won't have access to any of the things which you store in them. It is also worth checking that you have no

A puppy will soon look upon a crate as his own special den.

The toys you provide must be 100 per cent safe.

poisonous plants or shrubs in the garden. Care needs to be taken with ponds and water features, not only so that the puppy can't fall in the pond, but also so that he can't reach any electric cables which could be chewed. The latter also applies to the cables on your household appliances.

SLEEPING QUARTERS

To start off with it is better to use a plastic bed, as they can't be destroyed as easily as some of the others on the market. There are some lovely, comfy-looking beds available, but until you know how much your puppy or older dog will chew, it is safer and cheaper to stick to a plastic one, with a fleece or piece of blanket for him to lie on. Situate the bed in a quiet corner where the puppy won't need to be disturbed all the time.

INDOOR CRATE

If you decide to use a crate it will become your puppy or dog's bedroom, a place where your puppy can go to rest safely and without interference whenever he chooses or when he needs his sleep. Try to avoid crates with too big a gap between the wires, as your puppy or dog could get his feet, legs or mouth stuck between the bars. Dog crates, cages or indoor kennels are readily available now and when used correctly, they become a secure place where your puppy can feel safe and happy. Incorrectly used they can become a prison.

Have your crate ready for when you bring your puppy home. Site the crate in a busy part of the house so that your puppy is included in family life and can see what is going on. Make sure the location is

draught free, warm and light but avoid direct sunlight and really hot places. Line the bottom of the crate with newspaper in case of accidents. Put your puppy's bedding in the furthest end of the crate. If your puppy is very small, sometimes putting the bedding in a suitably sized cardboard box can help him to feel cosier, as to start with, he is bound to miss snuggling up together with his littermates. Put fresh water in a heavy bowl inside the crate, together with a toy and maybe some titbits, so that he realises that 'his bedroom' is a nice place to be.

Until family and friends are used to shutting gates and doors, and when boisterous children are around, the crate will be a place of safety. It must be big enough for your puppy or dog to move about comfortably inside. Always remove your puppy's collar before putting him in his crate, or he could get caught up and strangle himself.

A crate is a safe place in which to leave your puppy for *short* periods of time and also overnight. It will help with house training, as puppies do not like soiling where they sleep and will protect your puppy from harm when you cannot directly supervise him.

A crate should not be a place to lock up a dog or a puppy for hours on end (except overnight), a place to send your puppy as a punishment or a place in which to keep your puppy all the time.

A puppy's coat needs minimal grooming, but it is a good idea to get your pup used to being brushed.

TOYS

There is a very wide selection of toys available, but it is very important to remember the chew factor. Squeaky latex or fabric type toys should only be available to your puppy and dog when he is being supervised, as many dogs and puppies have been seriously ill through chewing and eating these types of toy. Hard rubber toys are much safer to be left with a puppy. The 'Kong' type ones are excellent for both puppies and older dogs, as they can be filled with a few treats or with part of the puppy's food and will provide your pet with plenty of fun as he tries to extract the food. Plastic milk bottles with the top removed, cardboard boxes or the inside tubes of kitchen rolls are also very good toys and cost nothing. Any balls used as toys should be large enough so that your puppy or dog can't swallow them or get

them lodged in their throat. Sticks should *never* be thrown as a retrieve toy for any dog, as they can cause serious damage and even death, if the end of the stick pierces the roof of the dog's mouth or his throat.

You will need three bowls. One food bowl, preferably stainless steel, as that is the easiest material to keep clean and sterilise and one heavy ceramic or stoneware bowl for water. The water bowl needs to be heavy to stop your puppy upsetting the water or trying to play with the bowl, which puppies quite often do with plastic ones. It is also a good idea to keep a third, small bowl in the car, so you will always have a drinking container when you have your dog travelling with you.

GROOMING EQUIPMENT

There are numerous types of dog brushes and combs on the

market, but the most useful for an adult Border Collie is a slicker brush, which has curved steel pins that can penetrate the dog's thick coat. You will also need a comb to use on the feathering behind the ears, one of the places where dogs are most likely to get matted hair. With a young puppy it is best to start off with a fairly soft nylon or bristle brush.

FINDING A VET

You will need to find a local vet and register your puppy or dog with them. Ask your family, friends or neighbours who have animals which vets they like best. Word of mouth is the best way to find a good vet in your area.

COLLECTING YOUR PUPPY

On the day your new puppy or dog is due to come to his new home, try to make arrangements to collect him in the morning, as this will give him more time to

COLLARS AND LEADS

You will need a collar and a lead for your puppy. Whilst he is still a puppy, a light nylon collar is probably best as these can easily be adjusted to fit. Your puppy will grow very quickly, so make sure you check regularly that the collar isn't becoming too tight for him. By law you will need an identity disc giving your contact details to attach to your puppy/dog collar. You will need a lead with which you feel comfortable. I prefer a soft leather lead, which is about four feet long, but try the leads out in the pet shop. There are a great variety available, so choose one which isn't going to slide through your fingers too easily and that is long enough to allow your puppy to walk comfortably.

If you are getting an older dog, ask advice from the breeder, owner or kennels as to the type of collar and lead the dog has been used to. Extendable leads are great for allowing your dog a little more freedom in safe open spaces, but they should not be used when walking a dog along on the pavement, as it is all to easy for the dog to stray on to the road if the lead is extended too far.

become accustomed to his new surroundings before he is left on his own for the night. If you have to collect the puppy or dog by yourself, make sure you have a crate or travelling box for him, as it can be very dangerous to travel with dogs loose in a car. When you collect your puppy ensure that you are given all the relevant paperwork, e.g. his pedigree, Kennel Club registration papers and any health clearance certificates that the puppy or his parents may have. It is also very important that you are given a diet sheet and information about the worming regime your puppy has had. If your puppy or dog has had any vaccinations, you should also be given a vaccination certificate. Most breeders will supply you with some of the food that your puppy or dog is being fed on, enough to last the puppy for several feeds. It is very important that you do not suddenly change the food that your puppy or dog has been eating, as this could cause an upset tummy. Any food changes should be done very gradually, over the course of a week to ten days.

ARRIVING HOME

When you arrive home, although it is very tempting to have all your family and friends round to meet your new pet, remember this is a very stressful and traumatic time for him and it is much better to keep things as quiet and peaceful as possible. As soon as you arrive home, let your puppy into the garden, stay with him and allow him to explore his new territory. It will give him a chance to go the toilet and get some fresh air, which will make him feel better after his journey in the car. Most puppies are car sick following their first few trips in the car, so don't worry if yours is. After he and you have spent 15 minutes or so in the garden, bring him indoors, but try and confine him to one room of the house to start with, as that will make it easier to cope with any accidents he might have and give him chance to get used to his new environment gradually. If you already have another dog, introduce the puppy and your resident pet in the garden, as some older dogs are frightened of puppies and it may take a few days for them to accept the new arrival. During this time make

Arriving in a new home is a daunting experience for a puppy. He needs a chance to explore his surroundings and to meet the family.

sure they are never left together unsupervised. Introductions to children and other pets should be done slowly and quietly, so as not to overwhelm the puppy, letting him get used to one new thing at a time. Make sure children are gentle with the puppy, just stroking him quietly, as he won't want to play until he is confident in his new surroundings.

Wait at least an hour before you offer your puppy any food and don't worry if he only eats a little of it. His life has undergone some major changes and it will take him a few days to adjust to them, so he maybe a little picky about his food. If you have taken on an older dog, check what time

he is used to being fed and try to stick roughly to that time at the start, as he may well go off his food for a few days as well.

If you have decided to use a crate for your Border Collie, let him spend the day getting used to it. Get your new pet used to entering the crate by putting either his food or a tasty titbit in the crate. Encourage him to go in by showing him the titbit, or play with one of his toys and keep throwing it in the crate.

Do not shut the door but let him become confident about going in and out of the crate before you close it. When he goes into the crate to eat or drink, praise him; when he is

sleepy try putting him in the crate and shutting the door for a few minutes. Gradually leave him in the crate for longer periods. Because puppies have a strong instinct not to foul their immediate environment, a crate is very helpful in house training. Your puppy will cry to be let out when he needs to relieve himself, giving you the opportunity to take him straight outside, supervise his toilet and praise him for being clean.

HOUSE TRAINING
House training should begin the day your puppy arrives. As he will relieve himself frequently, you will probably have a few

Do not worry if your puppy does not eat all his food to begin with.

accidents to begin with, but you should never punish the puppy as this could cause submissive urination when you tell him off. Most of the success will depend upon how well you can judge when your puppy needs to go to the toilet. Times to watch for are when your puppy first wakes up, immediately after eating, after playing and when he gets excited. Some dogs circle around several times and/or sniff the floor before they go to the toilet. If you see your puppy doing this, just quietly go outside with him, wait for him to relieve himself and then praise him for being a 'good boy'. Take him out at regular intervals to try to avoid accidents. Never put your puppy out alone and just leave him there unsupervised. You

need to go out with him too, whatever the weather, so that you can praise him as soon as he does his toilet. Use a specific phrase to encourage him to go to the toilet, such as 'be clean', 'hurry up' or whatever you decide. Most dogs will use the same area of the garden all the time, so try to work out which is his toilet area and encourage him to go there.

After a few weeks you will recognise what your dog does to let you know he needs to be let out – he may run around in circles next to the door which he knows he will go out of to relieve himself, he may bark or whine at the door, or just sit there or scratch at it. Dogs vary on what they do to let you know when they need to be let out for

the toilet, so you will just need to study your puppy until you realise what he does to alert you.

THE FIRST NIGHT

Most puppies will cry or whine for a while after being left for the first time on their own. Try not to keep going back to reassure him, as this will just make matters worse. Once the puppy realises that as soon as he makes a noise you will come back to him, he is not going to stop. Make sure your Border Collie has had a good run in the garden before you go to bed and that he has been quite active during the evening. Leave on a dim light and also a radio playing softly, so that the house doesn't suddenly go quiet. If your puppy is sleeping in a crate and he starts to make a noise during the night, it will probably be because he needs to go outside to toilet. Even in the middle of the night you must go out with him, so that you can see what he is doing and praise him as soon as he has performed.

HOUSE RULES

Right from the start you should have house rules for your puppy, such as not climbing on the furniture. If your Border Collie climbs on the chairs or sofa tell him "No" in a firm voice and put him on the floor, then give him one of his toys to play with. All the family must do this, as it is no good you telling the puppy not to climb on the furniture and other members of the family encouraging him to do so.

House rules must also apply to the whole family regarding keeping possessions in a safe place, out of reach of the puppy. He will not understand that your best shoes, gloves etc. are not toys, so it is up to you and your family to put your precious items in a safe place, where your puppy can't reach them.

PLAY BITING

Play biting should also be discouraged right from the start. Most puppies 'play bite'. It is quite natural; it is their way of finding out about things.

If you watch a litter of puppies, play biting is exactly what they do to each other. In that way they sort themselves out in to a pecking order, at the top of which is their Mum. In their early days, the puppies are

allowed to do what they like, but as they grow up, their mother and littermates alike become increasingly intolerant of sharp teeth. In that way the puppies learn that other individuals react to their biting behaviour and they learn to control the strength they use. Once your puppy is home, the pack leader needs to be you, so you must take over where your puppy's littermates and mother left off. Your puppy needs to be taught what is acceptable behaviour and what is not.

Play biting is very painful and should not be encouraged once your puppy is in his new home. It is often worse if a puppy is over-tired or over-excited, in which case you need to try to calm him down. He may simply need to go to the toilet or have a

For the first few nights a puppy is bound to miss the companionship of his littermates.

Divert your puppy's attention from inappropriate behaviour by giving him something positive to do.

sleep in his own space. If your Border Collie is getting too excited, try giving him a 'time out' spell by putting him in the garden on his own for a short while to give him a chance to calm down. If that does not work, you could offer an alternative 'plaything' by diverting his attention from your fingers, hands, feet, trousers or whatever he has decided will be fun to chew. A puppy will be attracted by anything which catches his eye, no matter what it is. One of the worst things you can do is to snatch your fingers or feet away quickly, as that will interest him even more.

Puppies can only concentrate on something for a very short period, so try attracting his attention to a ball on a rope, a tuggy, a knotted sock or any other favourite toy. This will usually work. (However, if you play tug-of-war with a pup, bear in mind that you need to 'win' any games you play together).

Alternatively, try to give your puppy something positive to think about and do, such as a puppy recall, a 'sit' or a 'down', so that you can praise him for being clever rather than nagging him for doing something which you consider to be wrong. It is not wrong to the puppy, who just does not know by what rules you want him to play at this stage in his life. It is your job to teach him!

Getting cross and losing your temper does not work, although sometimes saying "Ouch!" in the same tone you would use if you had hurt yourself can be effective. Using the word "No!" in a firm voice and giving the puppy a quick shake by the scruff of the neck can also work. If you use this approach, follow up the single verbal exclamation by ignoring the pup completely for a few seconds. In that way, you have stopped the game in the same way that his littermates would.

Remember to praise and reward your puppy for doing

A puppy is very quick to learn – and this includes picking up both good and bad habits.

what you want, rather than telling him off for showing what *you* consider to be inappropriate behaviour. A puppy would much rather please you than not and will learn your rules quicker with well-timed praise.

EARLY LEARNING

Get your puppy used to being groomed by brushing him for a few minutes each day. If you leave the grooming until he is tired after a good play or run around, he will be much happier to keep still and relax. This is a very important part of your dog's education and will give you a good chance to check him over for parasites, lumps and

bumps or anything out of the ordinary. Accustom your puppy to having his ears examined and having the pads on his feet checked over.   When a puppy is teething, he won't like having his mouth checked as his gums and mouth can be quite sore at this time, so it is best only to check mouths very gently, once a week. If your dog gets used to being handled and checked over on a regular basis, it will make visits to the vet a lot easier.

The first car journey your puppy had will probably have been very traumatic for him, as it will be the one when you collected him. He will remember it as being removed from his

brothers and sisters, taken away by strangers into a completely different world than that he has known before, so you are going to need to reassure him about the car in future. Start by placing him in the car for five or ten minutes while it is stationary, give him a few titbits and talk quietly to him. This way he will start to consider the car as a good place to be. Do this for several days, then make very short journeys with him, no longer than ten minutes to start with and gradually increasing the distance you travel. Some puppies and dogs can be very travel sick and it will be a case of perseverance. Try feeding your

HANDLING

Accustom your puppy to all-over handling so that he is happy to be groomed and will co-operate if he needs to be examined by a vet.

Check his ears to make sure they are clean.

Examine the teeth and gums.

Pick up each paw in turn.

Run your hands over the rear end going right to the tip of the tail.

If you take on an older dog, you will need to help him to settle into his new home.

puppy in the car, with the engine running while the car is stationary. The more time you spend reassuring your Border Collie that the car is a nice place to be, the better the chances of him being a good traveller.

When he is in the car he should always be confined, either in a crate or by a safety harness. Never travel with your Border Collie loose, for your own safety as well as that of the dog.

The most important thing to remember is *never leave your dog or puppy shut in the car in hot weather.* The inside of a car can become extremely hot even on mildly warm days and the suffering caused to dogs left in hot cars is horrific.

THE BEST OF CARE

5 Chapter

Those of us who own Border Collies love them very dearly, but showing affection is not enough. We show love for our dogs by giving them the best of care. They are totally dependent on their human friends to provide for all of their needs in the areas of food, grooming, comfort, exercise, security and affection. Ownership of any breed of dog brings these responsibilities, but the Border Collie is a very active and intelligent dog who deserves our highest commitment and will more than handsomely repay the love and care we offer. The more you come to know and love your Border Collie, and perhaps begin to meet others of the breed, you will be struck by how highly individual each one is. Caring for your dog as an individual is paramount. A Border Collie is not a "one size fits all" kind of dog.

What suits one may not suit another. Getting to know your own dog is a very rewarding experience.

FEEDING A BORDER COLLIE

A vital part of caring for your dog is providing food and fresh water. At first your puppy will be on three or four meals a day, but this will gradually reduce to one or two meals per day at around eight months of age.

Wherever possible, continue to feed the diet first provided by the breeder and take their advice on how much to feed and how often. If for reasons of finance or personal preference, you choose to change to another brand or different feeding menu, then the change must be gradual over 7 to 10 days, as otherwise serious tummy upsets will result. Whatever you choose to feed, it is vital for the healthy and steady growth of the young Border

Collie that you always keep in mind the ideal balance of protein, fats, carbohydrates, minerals and fibre required for your individual dog, and the amount of energy he or she will require at that stage of development.

- **Proteins:** These contain amino acids which are vital for growth and development. They mostly come from a meat or fish source as dogs find these almost 100 per cent digestible, whereas vegetable protein is anywhere from 20 to 30 per cent less digestible. In fact too much vegetable protein can lead to severe stomach upsets.
- **Fats:** These are easily digested by dogs and help create a significant amount of energy, plus being a carrier of essential vitamins. Fats also play an important role in making food more palatable as well as providing a healthy coat and sound nervous system.

The aim is to provide a well-balanced diet that is suited to a dog's individual energy needs.

- **Carbohydrates:** These are totally missing from fresh meat and fish plus 'all meat' tinned or frozen food but are present in dried foods in a balanced proportion.
- **Minerals:** Phosphorus and calcium are vital in your dog's diet, as both are needed for proper bone development in the puppy and young dog, plus a healthy balance of Vitamin D is needed throughout your dog's life. These minerals have to be very carefully balanced, not too much, nor too little. Too little calcium versus phosphorus will mean that bones will not develop strongly and may be brittle. Too much calcium can create bone deformities and may even stunt growth. The amount of calcium in complete foods is very carefully balanced, so do not be tempted to use supplements.
- **Fibre:** This is usually included as an ingredient in prepared foods as it aids the digestive process by passing food through the stomach more quickly. This can reduce stomach discomfort and prevent flatulence.

CHOOSING A DIET
When choosing a diet for your Border Collie, you should weigh up the pros and cons of what is available.

COMPLETE
Complete foods in the form of kibble have improved enormously in the last few years and are scientifically formulated to create an ideal, balanced diet. Under most circumstances, whether your dog is high energy or a couch potato, there will be a complete food which provides the calories and nutrition required to meet his needs.

CHOOSING A DIET

Canned food and biscuit.

Complete feed: This fulfils all your dog's nutritional requirements.

Homemade diet.

Crunching the kibble is beneficial for teeth and jaws, so do not moisten complete food once your young dog has his adult teeth, nor should you add meat or the nutritional balance will be adversely affected. If you really must add canned meat, it should be no more than 10 per cent of the meal, because the phosphorus which it contains will reduce the benefit of the calcium.

Feeding instructions and details of the ingredients are printed on the packaging and most companies also have an owners' helpline. For this reason, complete foods are the ideal choice for the new Border Collie owner, and they also have the advantage of being more user-friendly when you take your dog on holiday or board him at kennels.

CANNED

Canned meat and biscuit mixer is a popular choice with many owners. It is important to realise that there are at least two different types of canned dog food. Some are complete with no need to add mixer, others are meat only and must have mixer added to provide a balanced meal. Full instructions are found on the cans. Although not quite so easy to feed when travelling, it is another simple choice.

HOMEMADE

Over recent years there has been a slight increase in feeding dogs on homemade diets and bones. If you bought your puppy from a breeder who advocates this diet then, hopefully, you will have been supplied with menus and instructions. Particular care is required when feeding pups and

young dogs and yet again, it is the importance of ensuring the correct amount of calcium for growing bones – not too little and not too much. Your breeder may recommend the use of vitamins and minerals to make up for any lack in the diet and these should be used with great care. You may occasionally have to resort to another form of feeding, as it is very difficult to maintain standards when away from home or using boarding kennels.

All dogs will occasionally enjoy cooked chicken or scrambled egg, particularly if they are feeling off colour. Meaty bones can be given, always raw. Be aware that if bones are really small, some Border Collies will just swallow them whole without bothering to chew and this can cause severe abdominal blockage or puncture.

DANGERS OF OBESITY

Whatever you choose to feed, it is vital that your Border Collie does not become overweight; a simple test will help you to tell if he is in shape. You should be able to feel his ribs with just a light covering and, looking from above the dog, you should see his waist. Then he is in ideal condition. If you can't feel the ribs and your dog has a 'beer belly', then reduce the amount fed by 10-15 per cent for two weeks and then check again.

Don't forget that snacks and training treats can be high in calories, so take these into account. An adult male should weigh approximately 20 to 23 kg (44-51 lb) and a female between 15 and 20 kg (33-44 lb)

An obese dog is more prone to hip dysplasia, muscle and tendon injuries, diabetes and heart disease. If you want your dog to have a healthy happy life then he must be kept to a healthy weight.

GROOMING

A very important part of caring for your Border Collie is keeping him clean and tidy. Grooming is something your dog will enjoy and it should be started when your pup is at an early age. Your puppy will enjoy being brushed, so make it a special occasion rewarding him with treats when he allows you to brush him gently. This is extremely important as some dogs will resent being brushed as adults if they have not been properly introduced to grooming as a pup.

COAT CARE

Once your dog has grown a full coat, it will require regular brushing for a few minutes once or twice a week. This is required to remove any dirt and loose hair, plus promote a healthy coat. If

you can groom your dog every day, so much the better. Pay particular attention to the coat behind the ears, the tail and the trousers as this is where knots usually occur. Male dogs are particularly adept at creating knotted areas around their private parts, on the stomach and on the inner thigh.

The first brush to use on your puppy should be a medium soft bristle brush, but once the adult coat has developed then other tools will be required. The first of these is a pin brush, which has metal pins with rounded ends. The pins should be long enough to go through every layer of your dog's coat. The round ends prevent the pins from scratching his skin. If you encounter any knots then hopefully, they can be teased out with a comb. A comb

with rotating teeth is most useful as it does not tug and tear the coat. Stubborn knots may need to be very carefully cut out with round-ended scissors. Finally, a brush all over with a stiff bristle brush will complete the final touches and bring shine to a healthy coat.

TRIMMING

The Border Collie's coat does not require clipping. However, show dogs have the hair around their feet and pasterns and between the pads, trimmed to show off the athletic construction of the herding dog's feet. This procedure is well worth following with a pet, as it greatly reduces the amount of mud brought into the house and it also makes it easier to clean the feet and check for cuts or any other problems.

GROOMING A BORDER COLLIE

Before you start grooming, spray the coat with water which will make it easier to use a brush and comb through the hair.

A comb is needed for the feathering on the ears, gently teasing out any mats or tangles.

Comb through the feathering on the front legs, and then work along the undercarriage to the coat on the hindquarters.

The tail will need special attention.

Now brush the coat using a stiff, bristle brush.

Brush the body coat.

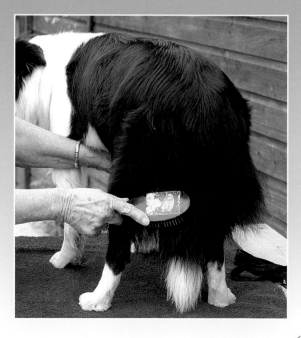

Work your way round
to the hindquarters.

TRIMMING

The show dog is lightly trimmed to enhance his appearance.

The hair behind the ears is thinned.

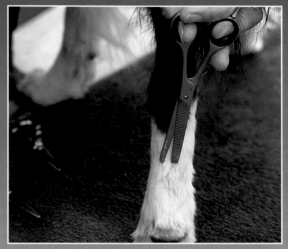

The hair on the back of the hocks is tidied up to give a smooth outline.

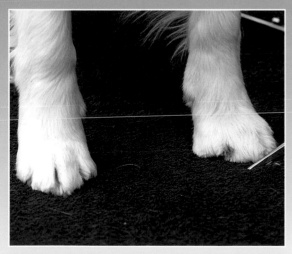

The hair around the feet is trimmed to give a neat cat-like appearance.

The hair that grows between the pads is trimmed.

The Border Collie is surprisingly good at keeping clean.

BATHING
Your Border Collie should be bathed now and again as a puppy to accustom him to the procedure. This is the stage of life at which your dog will probably be most in need of baths, because of toilet training accidents. The adult dog should not need so many baths but much depends on your lifestyle. A show dog will have to be bathed more often and so will those trained as therapy dogs who visit patients in hospitals. For a pet, a bath every three months will suffice if regular grooming is followed.

Human shampoo is unsuitable for dogs, as the type of hair is totally different. A wide range of dog shampoos are available from pet shops or supermarkets, and you will find a staggering array at dog shows. Do not use more shampoo than necessary and just smooth it into the coat without rubbing hard. Rinse very thoroughly.

It is amazing how a Border Collie can manage to keep his white parts so white, given his active lifestyle, but somehow even the filthiest dog will look better very quickly once the mud has dried and been brushed or licked off.

EARS
While you are grooming your Border Collie, check that his ears are clean. They can be gently wiped on the inside with a damp cloth. Never be tempted to use small cotton buds as they can easily slide into the delicate inner ear and cause severe problems which may require emergency veterinary assistance. If the ears are very dirty, you can buy specially formulated cleaners from your vet. If the ears are smelly, the problem may be canker requiring treatment with medicated drops. There may be a grass seed or some object trapped in the inner ear – in this instance the foreign body will need to be removed under general anaesthetic.

NAILS
Toenails should not be allowed to grow too long, and so they may need to be clipped. Dogs exercised on hard surfaces often keep their own nails short, However, you will need to check on the dew claw, which is located on the inner front foot in the position of a thumb, as it will grow into a hook and can catch

TEETH AND NAILS

If the nails do not wear down naturally, they will need to be clipped.

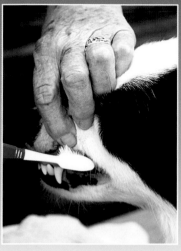

Regular brushing will keep the teeth clean and the gums healthy.

If necessary, tartar can be removed with a tooth scaler.

on surfaces causing injury.

A variety of canine nail clippers can be bought, which resemble secateurs or guillotines. If the nails are very long, you will have to use nail clippers, but there is always a danger of trimming the nail too far back and cutting into the quick which will bleed and be very painful. Professionals often use nail clippers, but if you are lacking in experience and the nails are not too long, we recommend that you use clippers designed for humans and simply 'nibble' back the nails to just short of the quick.

TEETH
Your Border Collie's teeth may need occasional cleaning. Again, begin this at an early age with a

very soft brush or even a rag wrapped around your finger. Never use human toothpaste, because it foams and the dog cannot either spit it out or swallow it down. Choose one of the delicious doggy varieties of toothpaste available at your pet shop or vet.

TRAVELLING
Your dog will love going on holiday with you, or going for an outing to the park or beach. Most breeders will have started to introduce young puppies to new experiences, including travelling in the car, but some young dogs may have problems with your particular car or even your style of driving. The first few journeys will create impressions in your

dog's mind so these should be very positive experiences. Ensure your Border Collie is comfortable and secure. Again, a dog crate is strongly recommended or you could have a dog guard fitted to prevent your dog jumping into the front of the car.

You should be fully prepared for the youngster who forgets his toilet training or is car sick. Carry a couple of refuse bags, disposable gloves, paper towels, nappy sacks and wet wipes plus old newspapers. If your dog has made a mess, do not scold him but just quietly clean up and pop him on fresh newspaper. Yes, you may feel cross but keep it to yourself. The more calmly you deal with problems the more your dog will trust you.

Planning a treat at the end of a journey, such as a run on the beach, may be the solution to travelling problems.

Perhaps you have taken on a rescued dog which has not been adequately socialised, and he may bark when in the car. Set aside time to deal with the problem in simple stages as you would with a puppy. Take it step by gentle step so you will be able to build up his confidence and travelling together will be a joy.

Despite all of your efforts you may have a dog which remains convinced that a car is to be avoided as it can only mean a trip to the vet. Our first Border hated the car. He had to be heaved into it and was constantly sick with fear. Our holiday destination was a two-hour drive away and we were determined to get him there. At least five stops were needed to clean him up and we became quite discouraged. On arrival we walked him on the beach and let him chase waves. He had a wonderful time. Returning to the car park, he jumped into the car and from that day on he was a problem-free traveller, always eager for the next adventure. All of our other dogs have been very quick to appreciate travelling with us and most people who own Border Collies have happy, confident travelling companions. If your dog has serious problems then speak to your vet about the wide range of solutions that are available.

If you are going on a long journey, always take fresh water and a bowl and try to stop every couple of hours. When you reach your hotel or holiday cottage, have a good look round before introducing your dog to his new environment, ensuring that he will be as safe from harm there as he is at home. He will be glad to see that you remembered to bring his bedding, bowls and favourite food.

GOOD AMBASSADORS
Whether you are on holiday or nearer home, it should be one of life's great pleasures to walk your Border Collie, but please don't forget that they all have some inherited instinct to chase

It is imperative to keep your Border Collie under control when he is free running.

and herd. Unless your dog is 100 per cent obedient to your every command, it is imperative to keep your dog on a lead when near livestock or on a nature reserve.

Where it is impossible to exercise your dog off lead, then an extending lead can give your Border Collie a sense of freedom while still being under control. This type of lead is ideal in open spaces where it cannot become tangled up. Check the lead regularly for wear and tear, and ensure that it is strong enough for the weight of your dog. A shorter lead is preferable in areas busy with traffic and people. It is the law in the UK that a dog has to be under control in a public

space. Some local authorities interpret that as 'on a lead'. If your Border Collie instinctively herds children, joggers or cars then a shorter lead is safer for all concerned.

As a general rule, Border Collies are very fastidious and can look quite embarrassed about going to the toilet in public, so they tend to squeeze their rear ends under something like a hedge, a rock or even a parked car. No matter where it lands it is your duty as his carer to clean it up. Always carry a good supply of poo bags. If you are squeamish about the task, then there are lots of gadgets designed to overcome your reservations.

SAFETY AND SECURITY

A vital part of caring for our dogs is to be constantly aware of their safety and security from puppyhood onwards throughout their lives. A Border Collie can make Houdini look like an amateur, particularly if you have left your dog behind and he wants to be with you.

A friend of ours left her young dog safely shut in her kitchen, so she was amazed to find him trotting down the lane towards her on her return. He had turned the handle on the door leading to the utility room where he jumped on to the washing machine, then slithered out of a very small window. Turning door handles is a popular trick with at least half

Your Border Collie should wear an ID tag, and, ideally, this should be backed up some form of permanent ID.

that they can be inserted at any stage in the dog's life, whereas a tattoo is usually applied in puppyhood. Whatever method you choose your vet or veterinary nurse will be happy to check that it is readable. On your dog's ID disc it will be useful to have the reverse side engraved with extra information such as your mobile phone number or your vet's number plus the words "ID Chip" or "Tattoo". If your dog is involved in an accident away from home and taken to a local vet, it will be possible for them to obtain from your own vet any information on your dog's medication or allergies.

FEMALE CARE

If your Border Collie is a bitch she will need more care and attention. In fact she will demand it, so don't expect to be let off lightly. Although there are exceptions, bitches tend to be more attentive and possessive towards their owners, snuggling up and pawing them for just one more cuddle. For this reason they are often seen as being better family pets than male Border Collies. Each sex has its own plus points and of course, each dog or bitch has his or her own virtues and faults as an individual. Your decision to have a bitch rather than a dog may perhaps be equally dependent on your own personality.

If you choose a female Border Collie, you take on an extra responsibility because for the whole of her life she will come into season and be capable of

the Border Collies that we know. If you have one of these geniuses, it is wise to change the handles on any doors that lead to danger zones. Round handles are best, or you could reverse the action of lever handles. If all else fails, fit a bolt. Often you will find that baby care stores have useful solutions for securing doors, windows, cupboards and fridges.

Caring for your Border Collie means ensuring, to the best of your ability, that he can never stray or be stolen from you. Keeping him safe and secure means never leaving him tied up outside a shop or in an unlocked

car. Your dog should always carry some form of identification. The law in the UK states that when in a public place a dog must wear a collar and ID tag. The tag should bear the owner's name, address and telephone number. Some other countries also insist that the dog is microchipped or tattooed. If your dog is lost or stolen, then his best chance of returning home lies in having these extra forms of identification.

Some people are unhappy about microchips and others say that tattoos can become illegible. Microchips have the advantage

There are health implications to be considered with neutering, so this option should be carefully considered if you do not want to breed from your Border Collie.

mating and having puppies. Unless you plan to breed from your bitch, you will have to take the utmost care to ensure she does not have an unwanted pregnancy. It is fashionable now to routinely spay a pet bitch to avoid all of the presumed problems that seasons can present, but such a decision should not be taken lightly. Unless you have an entire male dog in the house, or you lack the security to keep the local canine Romeo at bay, there is really no urgency about making the decision to spay or not.

A bitch in season should be kept safely in her own home, exercised in a secure garden, or popped in the car and taken to

an isolated beach or forest. If you think your bitch will run off, put her on an extending lead, but *never* walk her down your street unless you are inviting all the local dogs to follow you home and howl outside your window. Many boarding kennels have an isolation area for bitches in season and can provide a solution if you cannot care for your bitch personally.

If you are prepared to cope with your bitch's seasons, there is no reason to spay her at an early age. The chances of her having regular phantom pregnancies or pyometra or mammary tumours are mercifully uncommon, but spaying would become imperative under these circumstances. If you

decide to spay your bitch early in life you can avoid the above veterinary ailments, but you should be aware that, in some cases, the operation may create urinary incontinence which will exchange one problem for a greater one.

MALE CARE

As far as male Border Collies are concerned, the neutering operation, known as castration, is far less complex than spaying a bitch. However, it is not a decision that has to be made too early, unless you have an unspayed bitch in the house. Most well-behaved, house-trained dogs will not be a problem if they are left entire. Don't allow your

PLAY AND EXERCISE

The Border Collie thrives on regular and varied exercise combined with mental stimulation.

dog to roam the neighbourhood in search of a girlfriend. The motto with male dogs should be: "What they have never had they will never miss". Very occasionally an unlucky throw of the dice will produce a very macho dog which will scent mark by urinating on furniture. He would certainly be a candidate for castration in most homes. It is often claimed that neutering your dog will calm him down if he is over-excitable, but the operation is not always successful in modifying behaviour that has already become regular or ingrained.

If you are unsure about this aspect of castration, ask your vet about hormone injections which mimic the effects of the operation. If the injections don't work then neither will castration. Please don't routinely castrate a young dog that makes love to the vicar's leg – he will grow out of it, just don't encourage him by laughing out loud.

EXERCISING YOUR BORDER COLLIE

Breeders are often asked how much exercise will a Border Collie need. The public image of the breed is that of a high energy tornado excelling at Agility, Flyball or herding. To a certain extent it is true that most of them would enjoy these activities, given half a chance, because they possess the energy and stamina required. However, most breeders would stress that you must not over exercise your Border Collie while his bones are still growing and developing.

Playing a game of search or retrieve will give your Border Collie a chance to use his mind.

When you first take your puppy out and about after his vaccinations are complete, he can have a little stroll in the outside world, perhaps only of 10 minutes duration at first. Certainly up to the age of four months he should be walked no further than half a mile per day (i.e. quarter of a mile down and the same back home) on roads or hard surfaces. This may seem strange when the dear little pup is racing about everywhere in your garden, which leads you to believe he is tireless. But it is pounding along on hard roads or pavements which can cause bone damage in very young pups. After the age of four months the distance can be increased, but just gradually. Once your Border Collie is fully grown he will be happy with a daily walk of whatever distance you can

manage yourself because his favourite part of the walk is having you for company.

MENTAL STIMULATION

Although it is often said that Border Collies require a lot of exercise, most owners discover that what their dog needs most of all is mental stimulation. If that can be combined with physical exercise, then so much the better. Obedience training can never begin too early and it pays to join a local puppy training club which comes with a good recommendation. If you plan to show your Border Collie, you can join a ringcraft class which will teach you the tricks of the trade. If you bought your Border Collie with Agility in mind, he can be taught weaving poles and tunnels at an early age and master walking along a plank laid on the ground. Most Agility clubs will not allow dogs to jump more than a few inches until they are 15-18 months old, but of course, you can teach the word "Over" long before that if your dog has to jump over the doorstep or indeed over the cat.

Many people enjoy sports involving Frisbees, but again it is vital not to ask your Border Collie to jump high before his bones are of adult strength. By all means play with a Frisbee, but throw it low close to the ground while your dog is young and he will enjoy retrieving it. When he is old enough, then you can gradually increase the height.

Border Collies love to find things and can be taught to search at any age. Make it easy to begin with, perhaps hide a toy under a box letting the dog see what you are doing. Say "Find it!" in an excited tone and praise him hugely when he finds the toy. Gradually you can make the task more difficult and the objects more varied.

A very useful command to teach your Border Collie is "Hold it". Say the words in an encouraging tone each time he picks up a frisbee, a ball or even a toy and he will soon associate it with holding an object of any kind. From there it will be

An older dog deserves special care and consideration.

possible to teach catching and retrieving which will be a stepping stone in Obedience and Flyball. "Hold it" also has many domestic uses and your Border Collie can be trained to fetch the newspaper or help empty the washing machine. Anything which educates the mind of a Border Collie will help keep him out of mischief and build the bond between you.

CARING FOR THE OLDER DOG

The Border Collie is a very hardy breed and barring accidents and serious ailments, most dogs will usually live to an average age of around 13 years. Unless your old friend is a particularly grumpy geriatric, he will enjoy the

company of younger dogs and their zest for life.

The Border Collie tends not to complain much about the vicissitudes of life and so it is vital that the owner takes special care of the older dog. There are diets specially formulated for the veteran's teeth and digestion. Feeding these can greatly reduce the strain on older hearts and kidneys. Bones should not be given to old dogs as they encourage constipation.

Your dog may still be keen to go for his walks but he will become slower and not want to walk so far. Bear this in mind if you don't want to carry him home. If he is lame or cries out when exercised, then he must be in pain and your vet should be consulted. You may notice that your old friend does not see as well as he used to and it will be your responsibility to protect him. Don't move furniture out of the positions his mind will have mapped out or leave dangerous items lying around. He will enjoy taking longer naps in favourite spots and spending time with you just pottering around. He trusts you to have his wellbeing constantly at heart because you are his best friend and he is yours.

LETTING GO

As you see your dear Border Collie companion growing older or becoming ill, you will have the painful realisation that he will not be around forever. It will be natural for you to hope that he will simply close his eyes for a last sleep in his basket. Although that does happen, you will perhaps have to face a sad day when your dog collapses or when his medication is no longer helping, so euthanasia is the kindest choice.

Your love for your dog and his trust in you, will lead you to make the right decision to call the vet and to decide whether a home visit would be easier than a trip to the surgery. You will have time to say goodbye, telling your dog you will always remember what a marvellous friend he has been.

Of course you will be very sad and at first you will not know whether you want another Border Collie. In time, like many others before you, you will see that the greatest tribute we can pay to dogs we have loved and lost is to choose the companionship of another Border Collie. The new dog may not be a bit like his predecessor, but he will be privileged to have found such a caring and knowledgeable home – and you will love him to bits.

In time, you will be able to look back and remember all the happy times you spent with your beloved Border Collie.

TRAINING AND SOCIALISATION

Chapter 6

When you decided to bring a Border Collie into your life, you probably had dreams of how it was going to be: long walks together, cosy evenings with a Collie lying devotedly at your feet and whenever you returned home, there would always be a special welcome waiting for you.

There is no doubt that you can achieve all this – and much more – with a Border Collie, but like anything that is worth having, you must be prepared to put in the work. A Border Collie, regardless of whether it is a puppy or an adult, does not come ready trained, understanding exactly what you want and fitting perfectly into your lifestyle. A Border Collie has to learn his place in your family and he must discover what is acceptable behaviour.

The Border Collie is arguably the most intelligent breed of dog. The breed was developed to work as part of a team, in close communication with the shepherd, even when some distance away. He needed to be able to understand the sophisticated and complex work of herding, driving and penning, and the instructions given him by the shepherd either by speech or by whistle. He also needed to have the ability to process information very fast and react instantly to either sheep or shepherd.

The Border Collie has also developed the ability to work independently when out of contact with the shepherd and to 'know' what needs to be done without a direct instruction. The good working Collie can assess a situation and use his previous experience to deal with it. This ability has been developed on the

hills at distance from his handlers and having to deal with situations on his own.

The Border Collie now has a place as a highly valued companion dog, but he retains strong working instincts, which need to be channeled. This is a dog that thrives on using his brain – and it is your job to make sure he has the opportunity to do this.

THE FAMILY PACK

Dogs have been domesticated for some 14,000 years, but, luckily for us, they have inherited and retained behaviour from their distant ancestor – the wolf. A Border Collie may never have lived in the wild, but he is born with the survival skills and the mentality of a meat-eating predator who hunts in a pack. A wolf living in a pack owes its existence to mutual co-operation and an acceptance of a hierarchy, as this ensures both food and

Do you have what it takes to be a firm, fair and consistent leader?

protection. A domesticated dog living in a family pack has exactly the same outlook. He wants food, companionship and leadership – and it is your job to provide for these needs.

YOUR ROLE

Theories about dog behaviour and methods of training go in and out of fashion, but in reality, nothing has changed from the day when wolves ventured in from the wild to join the family circle. The wolf (and equally the dog) accepts a subservient place in the family pack in return for food and protection. In a dog's eyes, you are his leader and he relies on you to make all the important decisions. This does

not mean that you have to act like a dictator or a bully. You are accepted as a leader, without argument, as long as you have the right credentials.

The first part of the job is easy. You are the provider and you are therefore respected because you supply food. In a Border Collie's eyes you must be the ultimate hunter, because a day never goes by when you cannot find food. The second part of the leader's job description is straightforward, but for some reason we find it hard to achieve. In order for a dog to accept his place in the family pack, he must respect his leader as the decision-maker. A low-ranking pack animal does not question

authority; he is perfectly happy to see someone else shoulder the responsibility. Problems will only arise if you cut a poor figure as leader and the dog feels he should mount a challenge for the top-ranking role.

HOW TO BE A GOOD LEADER

There are a number of guidelines to follow to establish yourself in the role of leader in a way that your Collie understands and respects. If you have a puppy, you may think you don't have to take this on board for a few months, but that would be a big mistake. Start as you mean to go on and your pup will be quick to find his place in his new family.

- **Keep it simple:** Decide on the rules you want your Border Collie to obey and always make it 100 per cent clear what is acceptable and what is unacceptable behaviour.

- **Be consistent:** If you are not consistent about enforcing rules, how can you expect your Border Collie to take you seriously? There is nothing worse than allowing your Collie to jump up at you one moment and then scolding him the next time he does it, because you were wearing your best clothes. As far as the Collie is concerned, he may as well try it on because he can't predict your reaction.

- **Get your timing right:** If you are rewarding your Border Collie, and equally if you are reprimanding him, you must respond within one to two seconds otherwise the dog will not link his behaviour with your reaction (see page 83).

- **Read your dog's body language:** Find out how to read body language and facial expressions (see page 80) so that you understand your Collie's feelings and his intentions.

- **Be aware of your own body language:** You can help your dog to learn by using your body language to communicate with him. For example, if you want your dog to come to you, open your

Your dog will pick up signals from your body language.

arms out and look inviting. If you want your dog to stay, use a hand signal (palm flat, facing the dog) so you are effectively 'blocking' his advance.

- **Tone of voice:** Dogs are very receptive to tone of voice, so you can use your voice to praise him or to correct undesirable behaviour. If you are pleased with your Border Collie, praise him to the skies in a warm, happy voice. If you want to stop him raiding the bin, use a deep, stern voice when you say "No".

- **Give one command only:** If you keep repeating a command, or keep changing it, your Border Collie will

think you are babbling and will probably ignore you. If your Collie does not respond the first time you ask, make it simple by using a treat to lure him into position and then you can reward him for a correct response.

- **Daily reminders:** A young, exuberant Collie is apt to forget his manners from time to time, and an adolescent dog may attempt to challenge your authority (see page 98). Rather than coming down on your Collie like a ton of bricks when he does something wrong, try to prevent bad manners by daily reminders of good manners. For example:

i Do not let your dog barge ahead of you when you are going through a door.

ii Do not let him leap out of the car the moment you open the door (which could be potentially lethal, as well as being disrespectful).

iii Do not let your Border Collie eat from your hand when you are at the table.

iv Do not let him 'win' a toy at the end of a play session and then make off with it. You 'own' his toys, and you must end every play session on your terms.

UNDERSTANDING YOUR BORDER COLLIE

- Body language is an important means of communication between dogs, which they use to make friends, to assert status and to avoid conflict. It is important to get on your dog's wavelength by understanding his body language and reading his facial expressions.
- A positive body posture and a wagging tail indicate a happy, confident dog.
- A crouched body posture with ears back and tail down show that a dog is being submissive. A dog may do this when he is being told off or if a more assertive dog approaches him. Do not confuse this with posture of a 'working' Border Collie who will keep low to the ground, with his tail down. A working dog is alert and focused; a submissive dog is cautious and apprehensive. (See 'In Working mode').
- A bold dog will stand tall, looking strong and alert. His ears will be forward and his tail will be held high.

- A dog who raises his hackles (lifting the fur along his topline) is trying to look as scary as possible. This may be the prelude to aggressive behaviour, but in many cases, the dog is apprehensive and is unsure how to cope with a situation.
- A playful dog will go down on his front legs while standing on his hind legs in a bow position. This friendly invitation says: "I'm no threat, let's play."
- A dominant, aggressive dog will meet other dogs with a hard stare. If he is challenged, he may bare his teeth and growl and the corners of his mouth will be drawn forward. His ears will be forward and he will appear tense in every muscle (see page 100).
- A nervous dog will often show aggressive behaviour as a means of self-protection. If threatened, this dog will lower his head and flatten his ears. The corners of his mouth may be drawn back and he may bark or whine.
- Some Collies are 'smilers', curling up their top lip and showing their teeth when they greet people. This should never be confused with a snarl, which would be accompanied by the upright posture of a dominant dog. A smiling dog will have a low body posture and a wagging tail; he is being submissive and it is a greeting that is often used when low-ranking animals greet high-ranking animals in a pack.

Watch dogs meeting and greeting each other and you will learn to read their body language.

A Border Collie in typical working stance – tail down with head and shoulders stiff, ready for action.

IN WORKING MODE

When a Border Collie is herding sheep, he will adopt specific body postures that relate to the job he is doing. These classic postures, which have developed from the Border Collie's role as a herding dog, can all be seen to a greater or lesser degree in non-working Border Collies.

A good working dog will carry his tail down to give him balance and when he is in stalking mode, with head down and shoulders stiff, he has a quiet, steady, stalking pace enabling him to be ready for any situation. He can move an inch at a time, in apparent slow motion, or accelerate to chase at great speed. The key is to give no warning signals to the sheep. A young dog often has a gaily carried tail, a more upright stance and will hold his head up. With maturity, this type of dog may drop his tail as he becomes more experienced, but he is not likely to make as good a sheep working dog unless he does.

Often a Border Collie will lie down and watch, waiting for the right time to move. This is a key part of his herding behaviour and is used by shepherds to help pace the movement of the sheep, moment by moment.

Another breed characteristic of the Border Collie is his almost obsessive focus and concentration on the job in hand, and this intense focus is reflected in body posture. A Border Collie who has never met a sheep in his life still demonstrates these postures, which often can be used as an indicator of his personality, his ability to focus on the job in hand and his individual need to 'work' in some way.

This intense focus, which is a characteristic of the breed, can be used to great advantage in Obedience and Agility training, as well as in Search and Rescue with his unflagging attention to the task in hand.

GIVING REWARDS

Why should your Border Collie do as you ask? If you follow the guidelines given above, your Collie should respect your authority, but what about the time when he has just spotted a

THE BORDER COLLIE 'EYE'

If you watch a Border Collie herding sheep, you will soon be aware of the power of his eye. Many hunting animals use 'eye' to some level or other, which gives them the extra advantage of getting nearer to their prey. It can be seen seen in hunting dogs who concentrate intensely, almost hypnotising their target as they stalk towards it. This ability would have been highly prized when dogs accompanied their first masters on hunting expeditions and equally, when dogs were used for herding stock. The dogs with the best ability to use 'eye' would have been selected for breeding in the hope of strengthening the instinct as it was passed on to future generations.

A working Border Collie with a lot of 'eye' will try to gain control of the sheep simply by looking at them. It will pick out the lead sheep and its eyes will lock on and 'fasten' on to her. A dog with a lot of 'eye' is likely to have a strong working drive and puppies bred from two working dogs with a lot of 'eye' will not make easy family pets, unless living in an experienced household.

game of football or has found a really enticing scent? The answer is that you must always be the most interesting, the most attractive and the most irresistible person in your Collie's eyes. It would be nice to think you could achieve this by personality alone, but most of us need a little extra help. You need to find out what is the biggest reward for your dog – in a Border Collie's case, it will nearly always be a game with a special toy. Toys that involve play with the handler work well in building the relationship between dog and handler which then, as a side effect, can build the desire to please.

There are some dogs that care more about their stomachs and the biggest reward is a tasty food treat. It does not matter which type of reward you work with, but it must be something that your dog really wants. Some trainers use either food treats or a toy, depending on the exercise they are teaching. This also produces an element of surprise, which makes you appear even more interesting as a trainer!

When you are teaching a dog a new exercise, you should reward frequently. When your dog knows the exercise or command, reward him randomly so that he keeps on responding to you in a positive manner. If your dog does something extra special, like leaving a football game, make sure he really knows how pleased you are by having a really fun play session when he comes back to you, or giving him a handful of treats. If he gets a bonanza reward, he is more likely to come back on future occasions, because you have proved to be even more rewarding than his previous activity.

Most Border Collies see a game with a toy as the best reward.

MAKE IT SPECIAL

If you are using a toy as a reward, make sure you keep it exclusively for training sessions so that it has added value. In this way, your Border Collie will be really motivated to 'work' for his toy.

If you are using food rewards, you can grade your treats depending on what you are asking your dog to do. A dog may get a low-grade treat, such as a piece of dry food, to reward good behaviour on a random basis, such as sitting when you open a door or allowing you to examine his teeth. But high-grade treats, which may be cooked liver, sausage or cheese, are reserved for training new exercises or for use in the park when you want a really good recall.

When you are using food treats, remember to subtract the amount you are giving in training sessions from your Border Collie's daily ration. Fat Collies are lethargic, prone to health problems and will almost certainly have a shorter life expectancy. Reward your Collie, but always keep a check on his figure!

HOW DO DOGS LEARN?

It is not difficult to get inside your Border Collie's head and understand how he learns, as it is not dissimilar to the way we learn. Dogs learn by conditioning: they find out that specific behaviours produce specific consequences. This is known as operant conditioning or consequence learning. Consequences have to be immediate or clearly linked to the behaviour, as a dog sees the world in terms of action and result. Dogs will quickly learn if an action has a bad consequence or a good consequence.

Dogs also learn by association. This is known as classical conditioning or association learning. It is the type of learning made famous by Pavlov's experiment with dogs. Pavlov presented dogs with food and measured their salivary response (how much they drooled). Then he rang a bell just before presenting the food. At first, the dogs did not salivate until the food was presented. But after a while they learnt that the sound of the bell meant that food was coming, and so they salivated when they heard the bell. A dog needs to learn the association in order for it to have any meaning. For example, a dog that has never seen a lead before will be

THE CLICKER REVOLUTION

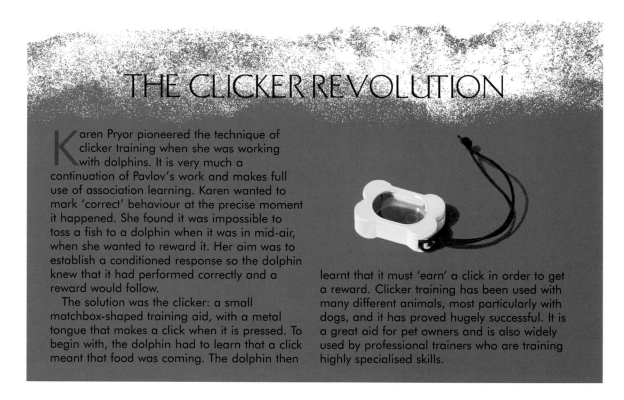

Karen Pryor pioneered the technique of clicker training when she was working with dolphins. It is very much a continuation of Pavlov's work and makes full use of association learning. Karen wanted to mark 'correct' behaviour at the precise moment it happened. She found it was impossible to toss a fish to a dolphin when it was in mid-air, when she wanted to reward it. Her aim was to establish a conditioned response so the dolphin knew that it had performed correctly and a reward would follow.

The solution was the clicker: a small matchbox-shaped training aid, with a metal tongue that makes a click when it is pressed. To begin with, the dolphin had to learn that a click meant that food was coming. The dolphin then learnt that it must 'earn' a click in order to get a reward. Clicker training has been used with many different animals, most particularly with dogs, and it has proved hugely successful. It is a great aid for pet owners and is also widely used by professional trainers who are training highly specialised skills.

completely indifferent to it. A dog that has learnt that a lead means he is going for a walk will get excited the second he sees the lead; he has learnt to associate a lead with a walk.

BE POSITIVE

The most effective method of training dogs is to use their ability to learn by consequence and to teach that the behaviour you want produces a good consequence. For example, if you ask your Border Collie to "Sit" and reward him with a treat, he will learn that it is worth his while to sit on command because it will lead to a treat. He is far more likely to repeat the behaviour, and the behaviour will become stronger because it results in a positive outcome. This method of training is known as positive reinforcement and it generally leads to a happy, co-operative dog that is willing to work and a handler who has fun training their dog.

The opposite approach is negative reinforcement. This is far less effective and often results in a poor relationship between dog and owner. In this method of training, you ask your Border Collie to "Sit" and if he does not respond, you deliver a sharp yank on the training collar or push his rear to the ground. The dog learns that not responding to your command has a bad consequence and he may be less likely to ignore you in the future. However, it may well have a bad consequence for you, too. A dog that is treated in this way may associate harsh handling with the handler and become aggressive or fearful. Instead of establishing a pattern of willing co-operation, you are establishing a relationship built on coercion.

GETTING STARTED

As you train your Border Collie, you will develop your own techniques as you get to know what motivates him. You may decide to get involved with clicker training or you may prefer to go for a simple 'command and reward' formula. It does not matter what form of training you use, as long as it is based on positive, reward-based methods.

There are a few important guidelines to bear in mind when you are training your Border Collie:

- Find a training area that is free from distractions, particularly when you are just starting out.
- Keep training sessions short, especially with young puppies that have very short attention spans.
- Do not train if you are in a bad mood or if you are on a tight schedule – the training session will be doomed to failure.
- If you are using food treats, make sure they are bite-size and easy to swallow; you don't want to hang about while your Collie chews on his treat.
- All food treats must be deducted from your Collie's daily food ration.
- When you are training, move around your allocated area so that your dog does not think that an exercise can only be performed in one place.
- If your Border Collie is finding an exercise difficult, try not to get frustrated. Go back a step and praise him for his effort. You will probably find he is more successful when you try again at the next training session.
- Always end training sessions on a happy, positive note. Ask your Border Collie to do something you know he can do – it could be a trick he

enjoys performing – and then reward him with a few treats or an extra-long play session. In the exercises that follow, clicker training is introduced and followed, but all the exercises will work without the use of a clicker.

INTRODUCING A CLICKER

This is really easy and a quick-witted Border Collie will learn about the clicker in record time! It can be combined with attention training, which is a very useful tool and can be used on many different occasions.

- Prepare some treats and go to an area that is free from distractions. When your Border Collie stops sniffing around

and looks at you, click and reward by throwing him a treat. This means he will not crowd you, but will go looking for the treat. Repeat a couple of times. If your Border Collie is very easily distracted, you may need to start this exercise with the dog on a lead.

- After a few clicks, your Border Collie understands that if he hears a click, he will get a treat. He must now learn that he must 'earn' a click. This time, when your Collie looks at you, wait a little longer before clicking and then reward him. If your Border Collie is on a lead but responding well, try him off the lead.
- When your Border Collie is

Find a training area that is free from distractions so your dog will give you his undivided attention.

You can use a treat or a toy to lure your dog into the Sit.

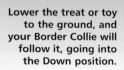

Lower the treat or toy to the ground, and your Border Collie will follow it, going into the Down position.

working for a click and giving you his attention, you can introduce a cue or command word, such as "Watch". Repeat a few times, using the cue. You now have a Collie that understands the clicker and will give you his attention when you ask him to "Watch".

• This is an invaluable exercise for the Border Collie, who can easily become fixated on something he finds of interest, which is in most cases, a moving object, such as a ball or a cyclist. If your Border Collie responds to the "Watch" command, you know you can

refocus his attention so that he concentrates on you (see page 81).

TRAINING EXERCISES

THE SIT
This is the easiest exercise to teach, so it is rewarding for both you and your Border Collie.

• Choose a tasty treat and hold it just above your puppy's nose. As he looks up at the treat, he will naturally go into the 'Sit'. As soon as he is in position, reward him.

• Repeat the exercise and when your pup understands what

you want, introduce the "Sit" command.

• You can practice mealtimes by holding out the bowl and waiting for your dog to sit. Most puppies learn this one very quickly!

THE DOWN
This is a natural position for the Border Collie so he should be quick to respond. Work hard at this exercise, because a reliable 'Down' is useful in many different situations and an instant 'Down' can be a lifesaver.

• You can start with your dog in a 'Sit', or it is just as effective to teach this when the dog is standing. Hold a treat just below your puppy's nose and then slowly lower the treat towards the ground. The treat acts as a lure and your puppy will follow it, first going down on his forequarters and then bringing his hindquarters down as he tries to get the treat.

- Make sure you close your fist around the treat and only reward your puppy with the treat when he is in the correct position. If your puppy is reluctant to go 'Down', you can place your hand on his shoulders to encourage him to go into the correct position.
- When your puppy is following the treat and going into position, introduce a verbal command.
- Build up this exercise over a period of time, each time waiting a little longer before giving the reward, so the puppy learns to stay in the 'Down' position.

THE RECALL

- It is never too soon to start training the Recall. Make sure you are always happy and excited when your Border Collie comes to you, even if he has been slower than you would like. Your Collie needs to believe that the greatest reward is coming to you.
- You can start teaching the recall from the moment your puppy arrives home. He will naturally follow you, so keep calling his name and rewarding him when he comes to you.

Practice Recalls in the garden to build up a reliable response.

- Practise in the garden and when your puppy is busy exploring, get his attention by calling his name. As he runs towards you, introduce the verbal command "Come". Make sure you sound happy and exciting, so your puppy wants to come to you. When he responds, give him lots of praise.
- If your puppy is slow to respond, try running away a few paces, or jumping up and down. It doesn't matter how silly you look, the key issue is to get your puppy's attention and then make yourself irresistible!
- In a dog's mind, coming when called should be regarded as the best fun because he knows he is always going to be rewarded. Never make the mistake of telling your dog off,

no matter how slow he is to respond, as you will undo all your previous hard work.

- When you are free running your dog, make sure you have his favourite toy or a pocket full of treats, so you can reward him at intervals throughout the walk when you call him to you. Do not allow your dog to free run and only call him back at the end of the walk to clip his lead on. An intelligent Border Collie will soon realise that the recall means the end of his walk and the end of fun – so who can blame him for not wanting to come back?

TRAINING LINE

This is the equivalent of a very long lead, which you can buy at a pet store, or you can make your own with a length of rope. The training line is attached to your

SECRET WEAPON

You can build up a strong recall by using another form of association learning. Buy a whistle and when you are giving your Border Collie his food, peep on the whistle. You can choose the type of signal you want to give: two short peeps, or one long whistle, for example. Within a matter of days, your dog will learn that the sound of the whistle means food is coming.

Now transfer the lesson outside. Arm yourself with some tasty treats and the whistle. Allow your Border Collie to run free in the garden and after a couple of minutes, use the whistle. The dog has already learnt to associate the whistle with food, so he will come towards you.

Immediately reward him with a treat and lots of praise. Repeat the lesson a few times in the garden so you are confident that your dog is responding, before trying it in the park. Make sure you always have some treats in your pocket when you go for a walk and your dog will quickly learn how rewarding it is to come to you.

Border Collie's collar and should be around 15 feet (4.5 metres) in length.

The purpose of the training line is to prevent your Border Collie from disobeying you so that he never has the chance to get into bad habits. For example, when you call your Border Collie and he ignores you, you can immediately pick up the end of the training line and call him again. By picking up the line you will have attracted his attention, and if you call in an excited, happy voice, your Collie will come to you. The moment he comes to you, give him a tasty treat, or produce his favourite toy so he is instantly rewarded for making the 'right' decision.

The training line is very useful when Border Collies become adolescent and are testing your leadership. When you have reinforced the correct behaviour a number of times, your dog will build up a strong recall and you will not need to use a training line.

WALKING ON A LOOSE LEAD
This is a simple exercise, which baffles many Border Collie owners. In most cases, owners are too impatient, wanting to get on with the expedition rather than training the dog how to walk on a lead. Take time with this one; a Border Collie can become addicted to straining on the lead and a Collie that pulls

on the lead is no pleasure to own.
- In the early stages of lead training, allow your puppy to pick his route and follow him. He will get used to the feeling of being 'attached' to you and will have no reason to put up any resistance.
- Next, find a toy or a tasty treat and show it to your puppy. Let him follow the treat/toy for a few paces and then reward him.
- Build up the amount of time your pup will walk with you and when he is walking nicely by your side, introduce the verbal command "Heel" or "Close". Give lots of praise when your pup is in the correct position.

The aim is for your Border Collie to walk on a loose lead, giving his attention when required.

With practice, your Border Collie will be rock steady in the Stay, even when you leave him at some distance.

- When your pup is walking alongside you, keep focusing his attention on you by using his name and then rewarding him when he looks at you. If it is going well, introduce some changes of direction.
- Do not attempt to take your puppy out on the lead until you have mastered the basics at home. You need to be confident that your puppy accepts the lead and will focus his attention on you when requested, before you face the challenge of a busy environment.
- As your Border Collie grows bigger and stronger, he may try to pull on the lead, particularly if you are heading somewhere

he wants to go, such as the park. If this happens, stop, call your dog to you and do not set off again until he is in the correct position. It may take time, but your Border Collie will eventually realise that it is more productive to walk by your side, than to pull ahead.

STAYS

This may not be the most exciting exercise, but it is one of the most useful. There are many occasions when you want your Border Collie to stay in position, even if it is only for a few seconds. The classic example is when you want your Collie to stay in the back of the car until you have clipped his lead on.

Some trainers use the verbal command "Stay" when the dog is to stay in position for an extended period of time and "Wait" if the dog is to stay in position for a few seconds until you give the next command. Other trainers use a universal "Stay" to cover all situations. It all comes down to personal preference, as long as you are consistent, your dog will understand the command he is given.

- Put your puppy in a 'Sit' or a 'Down' and use a hand signal (flat palm, facing the dog) to show he is to stay in position. Step a pace away from the dog. Wait a second, step back and reward him. If you have a lively pup, you may find it easier to train this exercise on the lead.

- Repeat the exercise, gradually increasing the distance you can leave your dog. When you return to your dog's side, praise him quietly and release him with a command, such as "OK".
- Remember to keep your body very still when you are training this exercise and avoid eye contact with your dog. Work on this exercise over a period of time and you will build up a really reliable 'Stay'.

SOCIALISATION

While your Border Collie is mastering basic obedience exercises, there is other equally important work to do with him. A Border Collie is not only becoming a part of your home and family, he is becoming a member of the community. He needs to be able to live in the outside world, coping calmly with every new situation that comes his way. It is your job to introduce him to as many different experiences as possible and encourage him to behave in an appropriate manner.

In order to socialise your Border Collie effectively, it is helpful to understand how his

Puppies learn vital lessons by interacting with each other, and with their mother.

brain is developing. You will then gain a perspective on how he sees the world.

PRIMARY SOCIALISATION (Birth to 8 weeks)

These weeks will be when the puppy is still with its breeder. Responsible breeders will ensure their puppies have gentle, daily handling and first introductions to new sights and sounds in a controlled and positive manner including playing with gentle children. Puppies are also learning from watching their mother during this time and watch how she reacts to noises, visitors and general household activities. These very early experiences help to build a very confident puppy that is ready to go to its new owners at 8 weeks. A puppy that has been kept with its mother away from general day to day

activities perhaps in a distant barn or kennel, miss these crucial opportunities for positive early lessons. This is one of the reasons that puppy farms are so damaging to the future life of a dog and should be avoided by all responsible owners.

This is the time when a dog learns how to be a dog. By interacting with his mother and his littermates, a young pup learns about leadership and submission. He learns to read body posture so that he understands the intentions of his mother and his siblings. A puppy that is taken away from his litter too early may always have behavioural problems with other dogs, either being fearful or aggressive.

SECONDARY SOCIALISATION PERIOD (8 to 12 weeks)

This is the time for you, as the new owner, to continue what the breeder has started. Introduce your Border Collie puppy to as many different experiences as possible. This includes meeting different people, other dogs and animals, seeing new sights and hearing a range of sounds, from the vacuum cleaner to the roar of traffic. At this stage, a puppy learns very quickly and what he learns will stay with him for the rest of his life. This is the best time for a puppy to move to a new home, as he is adaptable and ready to form deep bonds.

FEAR-IMPRINT PERIOD
(8 to 11 weeks)
This occurs during the socialisation period and it can be the cause of problems if it is not handled carefully. If a pup is exposed to a frightening or painful experience, it will lead to

As puppies start to grow up, they will question who is the pack leader.

lasting impressions. Obviously, you will attempt to avoid frightening situations, such as your pup being bullied by a mean-spirited older dog, or a firework going off, but you cannot always protect your puppy from the unexpected. If your pup has a nasty experience, the best plan is to make light of it and distract him by offering him a treat or a game. The pup will take the lead from you and will be reassured that there is nothing to worry about. If you mollycoddle him and sympathise with him, he is far more likely to retain the memory of his fear.

SENIORITY PERIOD
(12 to 16 weeks)
During this period, your Border Collie puppy starts to cut the apron strings and becomes more independent. He will test out his

status to find out who is the pack leader: him or you. Bad habits, such as play biting, which may have been seen as endearing a few weeks earlier, should be firmly discouraged. Remember to use positive, reward-based training, but make sure your puppy knows that you are the leader and must be respected.

SECOND FEAR-IMPRINT PERIOD *(6 to 14 months)*
This period is not as critical as the first fear-imprint period, but it should still be handled carefully. During this time your Border Collie may appear apprehensive, or he may show fear of something familiar. You may feel as if you have taken a backwards step, but if you adopt a calm, positive manner, your Border Collie will see that there is nothing to be frightened of. Do

not make your dog confront the thing that frightens him. Simply distract his attention and give him something else to think about, such as obeying a simple command, such as "Sit" or "Down". This will give you the opportunity to praise and reward your dog and will help to boost his confidence.

YOUNG ADULTHOOD AND MATURITY
(1 to 4 years)
The timing of this phase depends on the size of the dog: the bigger the dog, the later it is. This period coincides with a dog's increased size and strength, mental as well as physical. Some dogs, particularly those with an assertive nature, will test your leadership again and may become aggressive towards other dogs. Firmness and continued training are essential at this time so that your Border Collie accepts his status in the family pack.

IDEAS FOR SOCIALISATION
When you are socialising your Border Collie, you want him to experience as many different situations as possible. Try out some of the following ideas, which will ensure your Collie has an all-round education.

If you are taking on a rescued dog and have little knowledge of

A well socialised Border Collie will be an integral part of family life, taking all new situations in his stride.

his background, it is important to work through a programme of socialisation. A young puppy soaks up new experiences like a sponge, but an older dog can still learn. If a rescued dog shows fear or apprehension, treat him in exactly the same way as you would treat a youngster who is going through the second fear-imprint period (see page 91).

- Accustom your puppy to household noises, such as the vacuum cleaner, the television and the washing machine.
- Ask visitors to come to the door, wearing different types of clothing – for example, wearing a hat, a long raincoat, or carrying a stick or an umbrella.
- If you do not have children at home, make sure your Border Collie has a chance to meet and play with them. Go to a local park and watch children

in the play area. You will not be able to take your Collie inside the play area, but he will see children playing and will become used to their shouts of excitement.

- Attend puppy classes. These are designed for puppies between the ages of 12 to 20 weeks and give puppies a chance to play and interact together in a controlled, supervised environment. Your vet will have details of a local class.
- Take a walk around some quiet streets, such as a residential area, so your Border Collie can become used to the sound of traffic. The Border Collie can be more sensitive to sound than other breeds, so take your time with this and only progress to busier areas when he becomes more confident.
- Go to a railway station. You

don't have to get on a train if you don't need to, but your Border Collie will have the chance to experience trains, people wheeling luggage, loudspeaker announcements and going up and down stairs and over railway bridges.

- If you live in town, plan a trip to the country. You can enjoy a day out and provide an opportunity for your Border Collie to see livestock, such as sheep, cattle and horses. This is vitally important for the Border Collie, who has a strong instinct to herd and chase livestock. (See pages 81 and 96)
- One of the best places for socialising a dog is at a country fair. There will be crowds of people, livestock in pens, tractors, bouncy castles, fairground rides and food stalls.
- When your dog is over 20 weeks of age, find a training class for adult dogs. You may find that your local training class has both puppy and adult classes.

TRAINING CLUBS

There are lots of training clubs to choose from. Your vet will probably have details of clubs in your area, or you can ask friends who have dogs if they attend a club. Alternatively, use the internet to find out more information. But how do you know if the club is any good?

Before you take your dog, ask if you can go to a class as an observer and find out the following:

- What experience does the instructor(s) have?
- Do they have experience with Border Collies?
- Is the class well organised and are the dogs reasonably quiet? (A noisy class indicates an unruly atmosphere, which will not be conducive to learning).
- Are there are a number of classes to suit dogs of different ages and abilities?
- Are positive, reward-based training methods used?
- Does the club train for the Good Citizen Scheme (see below)?
- If you are not happy with the training club, find another one. An inexperienced instructor who cannot handle a number of dogs in a confined environment can do more harm than good.

Adolescence is a time when a dog will test his boundaries.

GOOD CITIZEN SCHEME
This is a scheme run by the Kennel Club in the UK and the American Kennel Club in the USA. The schemes promote responsible ownership and help you to train a well-behaved dog who will fit in with the community. The schemes are excellent for all pet owners and they are also a good starting point if you plan to compete with your Border Collie when he is older. The KC and the AKC schemes vary in format. In the UK there are three levels: bronze, silver and gold, with each test becoming progressively more demanding. In the AKC scheme there is a single test.

Some of the exercises include:
- Walking on a loose lead among people and other dogs.
- Recall amid distractions.
- A controlled greeting where dogs stay under control while owners meet.
- The dog allows all-over grooming and handling by its owner and also accepts being handled by the examiner.
- 'Stays' with the owner in sight and later, out of sight.

- Food manners, allowing the owner to eat without begging and taking a treat on command.
- 'Sendaway' – sending the dog to his bed.
- The tests are designed to show the control you have over your dog and his ability to respond correctly and remain calm in all situations. The Good Citizen Scheme is taught at most training clubs. For more information, log on to the Kennel Club or AKC website (see Appendices).

THE ADOLESCENT BORDER COLLIE
It happens to every dog – and every owner. One minute you have an obedient well-behaved youngster and the next you have a boisterous adolescent who appears to have forgotten everything he learnt. This applies equally to males and females, although the type of adolescent behaviour and its onset, varies between individuals.

Some lines mature more slowly than others, but as a general rule a bitch has come through adolescence and is showing her adult behaviour by the time she is 12 months old, whereas a dog may be slower to mature.

BONUS EXERCISES FOR BRAINY BORDER COLLIES

The Border Collie is a breed apart and we need to make special efforts to provide mental stimulation. You need to allocate small chunks of time every day, in which you can train or play games with your dog. If you are not planning on training your Border Collie as a working dog, there are lots of dog sports now that will introduce some challenge and give extra mental stimulation. These range from Obedience training to Agility and Flyball, and all the training that you do at home on a day to day basis will help keep your dog interested (see 'New Challenges').

Another way to channel the Border Collie's intelligence is to give him something extra to do in his everyday life. Teach him tricks and help him to join in with your everyday activities in some shape or form. Turn your dog into an assistance dog and teach him to help with the chores, for example, packing the children's toy box or training him to carry a brush upstairs for you.

Other ideas include:

- Teaching your dog to "Speak" and to be "Quiet". You can also teach him to use his voice in a trick situation, for example doing 'sums' and 'counting'. Training methods are shown in books on trick training,

- Teach your Border Collie to bark to tell you when the telephone rings, but make sure you teach him to be "Quiet" once he has alerted you to the call.

There are also many 'interactive' toys on the market which require the dog to work for food treats and can pose quite a challenge. Once again, the Border Collie shows his intelligence by easily mastering some of the most difficult toys available.

Remember, training is the best form of mental stimulation. The Border Collie will learn new exercises very quickly and will thoroughly enjoy showing off his skills,

Just like a teenager, an adolescent Border Collie feels the need to flex his muscles and challenge the status quo. He may become disobedient and break house rules as he tests your authority and your role as leader. When this happens, you need to go back a few steps in your training programme using extra positive reinforcement rather than becoming annoyed and frustrated, as this will only exacerbate the problem

As your Border Collie matures, he will become calmer and easier to handle, but do not assume inappropriate behaviour will evaporate when he is older. Ongoing training is crucial, as the longer a behaviour is ingrained, the harder it is to retrain. Do not allow a young dog to behave in a way that will be unacceptable when he is older. What seems cute in a small pup may be highly undesirable once he is full grown.

WHEN THINGS GO WRONG

Positive, reward-based training has proved to be the most effective method of teaching dogs, but what happens when your Border Collie does something wrong and you need to show him that his behaviour is unacceptable? The old-fashioned school of dog training used to rely on the powers of punishment and negative reinforcement. A dog who raided the bin, for example, was smacked. Now we have learnt that it is not only unpleasant and cruel to hit a dog, it is also ineffective. If you hit a dog for stealing, he is more than likely to see *you* as the bad consequence of stealing, so he may raid the bin again, but probably not when you are around. If he raided the bin some time before you discovered it, he will be even more confused by your punishment, as he will not relate your response to his 'crime'.

A more commonplace example is when a dog fails to respond to a recall in the park. When the dog eventually comes back, the owner puts the dog on the lead and goes straight home to punish the dog for his poor response. Unfortunately, the dog will have a different interpretation. He does not think: "I won't ignore a recall command because the bad consequence is the end of my play in the park." He thinks: "Coming to my owner resulted in the end of playtime – therefore coming to my owner has a bad consequence so I won't do that again."

There are a number of strategies to tackle undesirable behaviour – and they have nothing to do with harsh handling.

Ignoring bad behaviour: A lot of undesirable behaviour in a young Border Collie is to do with over-exuberance. This trait is part of the breed's charm, but it can lead to difficult and sometimes dangerous situations. For example, a young Collie that repeatedly jumps up at visitors will eventually knock someone over unless he is stopped. In this case, the Border Collie is seeking attention and so the best plan is to ignore him. Do not look at him, do not speak to him, and do not push him down – all these actions are rewarding for your Border Collie. But someone who turns their back on him and offers no response is plain boring. The moment your Collie has four feet on the ground, give him lots of praise and maybe a treat. If you repeat this often enough, the Collie will learn that jumping up does not have any good consequences, such as getting attention. Instead he is ignored. However, when he has all four feet on the ground, he gets loads of attention. He links the action with the consequence and chooses the action that is most rewarding. You will find that this strategy works well with all attention seeking behaviour, such as barking, whining or scrabbling

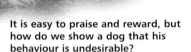

It is easy to praise and reward, but how do we show a dog that his behaviour is undesirable?

at doors. Being ignored is a worst-case scenario for a Border Collie, so remember to use it as an effective training tool.

Stopping bad behaviour: There are occasions when you want to call an instant halt to whatever it is your Border Collie is doing. He may have just jumped on the sofa, or you may have caught him red-handed in the rubbish bin. He has already committed the 'crime', so your aim is to stop him and to redirect his attention. You can do this by using a deep, firm tone of voice to say "No", which will startle him, and then call him to you in a bright, happy voice. If necessary, you can attract him with a toy or a treat. The moment your Border Collie stops the undesirable behaviour and comes towards you, you can

Ignoring your dog is an effective way of showing him that his attention seeking behaviour is not working.

reward his good behaviour. You can back this up by running through a couple of simple exercises, such as a 'Sit' or a 'Down' and rewarding with treats. In this way, your Collie focuses his attention on you and sees you as the greatest source of reward and pleasure.

In a more extreme situation, when you want to interrupt undesirable behaviour and you know that a simple "No" will not do the trick, you can try something a little more dramatic. If you get a can and fill it with pebbles, it will make a really loud noise when you shake it or throw it. The same effect can be achieved with purpose-made training discs. The dog will be startled and stop what he is doing. Even better, the dog will

not associate the unpleasant noise with you. This gives you the perfect opportunity to be the nice guy, calling the dog to you and giving him lots of praise.

PROBLEM BEHAVIOUR

We have already discussed the Border Collie's outstanding intelligence. But we need to bear in mind that intelligence can be a double-edged sword, as it can be used as a means of manipulation which can result in problems for an inexperienced owner. Sometimes problems arise unexpectedly, or maybe you have taken on a rescued Border Collie that has established behavioural problems.

If you are worried about your Border Collie and feel out of your depth, do not delay in seeking

professional help. This is readily available, usually through a referral from your vet, or you can find out additional information on the internet (see Appendices for web addresses). An animal behaviourist will have experience in tackling problem behaviour and will be able to help both you and your dog.

OBSESSIVE BEHAVIOUR

In the canine world, the Border Collie has an unparalleled ability to focus on a specific task. This is highly prized in a working dog, but if you are not rearing or training a dog as a working sheepdog, you need to be very careful about how you adapt this intense focus to things that you wish the dog to be 'obsessed' about. The exciting early games of fetch with a puppy can pall and lead to annoying, repetitive behaviour by a ball obsessed dog who repeatedly presents a toy to be thrown.

It is the strong working instincts – chasing, herding and nipping – that can become obsessive. A classic behavioral characteristic of hunting animals, is encircling and nipping the heels of members of the herd to contain them and hold them in position for the pack leader to make the 'kill'. The 'chase-nip' instinct is strong and much prized in certain lines of working dogs, particularly dogs that are working both cattle and sheep.

In a family situation however, a dog with a strong working instinct will start to herd family members, cars, cats, cyclists, joggers – in fact anything that moves, even sunbeams or insects. Some chase toys, such as balls or frisbees, in an obsessive way that stops them interacting well with the family. This herding behaviour may involve encircling, chasing and nipping people or cars with potentially fatal consequences for the dog.

Some trainers believe that it is important to try to counteract the chase instinct of a Border Collie, by banning ball games involving a ball being chased, until the dog is over two years. One technique is to restrain the dog in a 'Wait' or to use the command "Leave" until the ball has settled and then to send the dog to fetch the ball. If you want to channel the chase instinct rather than inhibit it, train your dog in Flyball where

If chasing behaviour gets out of hand, it can have disastrous consequences.

the chase response is encouraged – and is an important part of why the Border Collie excels at the sport.

Playing hide and seek is a positive way of preventing your dog becoming ball obsessed. You can hide a variety of toys – cat nip toys are a favourite – and encourage your Border Collie seek them out. If you have children, they can hide, and your Collie can become a search and rescue dog for the family.

It is important to be 100 per cent consistent in encouraging the behaviour you want and preventing the behaviour you do not want. For example, if your Border Collie gets away with chasing a squirrel or the neighbour's cat, you should not be surprised if he decides to chase bikes or joggers.

It is vital to supervise interactions with young children and to teach children how to play safely with the puppy. If a child runs away from a puppy, waving their arms and squealing in a high-pitched voice, it will encourage the pup to chase. It might then bring out the chase and nip side of his instinct, which could prove disastrous. If a dog has not had the experience of interacting with calm, sensible children in his early weeks, he is less likely to become a good family dog. 'Unlearning' chasing children is more difficult than avoiding it in the first place. The excitement of the chase is something a dog will want to repeat once he has experienced it.

The behaviour of a dog that is constantly wanting to 'round up' people is particularly suitable to be channeled into Heelwork To Music and Dancing With Dogs as a hobby. Many of the movements involve the dog going round his partner and lying down. In this way you are controlling his instinctive behaviour and adapting it in something that can become a good social activity for both owner and dog.

SEPARATION ANXIETY

If your Border Collie is brought up to accept short periods of separation from his owner, there is no reason why he should become anxious. A new puppy should be left for short periods on his own, ideally in a crate where he cannot get up to any mischief. When you return, do not rush to the crate and make a huge fuss. Wait a few minutes and then calmly go to the crate and release your dog, telling him how good he has been. If this scenario is repeated a number of times, your Border Collie will soon learn that being left on his own is no big deal.

The Border Collie is a highly intelligent dog and there is a danger that he will become bored when he is left, which could lead to undesirable behaviour, such as barking and whining. The best way to overcome this potential problem is to leave your Border Collie with a boredom busting toy, such as a 'Kong' stuffed with food, so he will be happily occupied in your absence.

Dogs that show anxiety may have been taken from their mother too early. A pup's early weeks are a key part of his socialisation and the mother's response to visitors, noises and everything that happens, gives the pup a lead on what to take in his stride and what to be fearful of. A pup that is not reared by a calm mother with a sound temperament may be fearful of new situations simply because he is experiencing them at a different and later developmental stage without any lead from his mother. This type of dog is more likely to become anxious long

term and will need considerable re-training to overcome his fears. In the formative weeks of a pup being reared in the home rather than in a barn distant from people, he also learns who is the pack leader by watching his mother's reactions and responses.

It is possible to manage separation anxiety by developing a signal which shows the dog that you will be returning. Practice leaving your dog safe in his crate with something to occupy him like a toy or chew and place an item, for example a can of baked beans, in view of the dog. Leave the room and when you come back, put the baked bean can back in the cupboard before greeting the dog. If regularly repeated, the dog learns that when the can of beans is in view you are absent, but the sequence of events has not been completed until you return and put the can away. In this way, the can becomes a signal showing that you will be coming back.

ASSERTIVE BEHAVIOUR

If you have trained and socialised your Border Collie correctly, he will know his place in the family pack and will have no desire to challenge your authority. As we have seen, adolescent dogs test the boundaries and this is the time to enforce all your earlier training so your Border Collie accepts that he is not top dog.

Within each litter there are pups with varying levels of assertiveness and this will be reflected later in life. However, if the owner is very submissive,

A boredom busting toy will help to occupy your dog's mind.

quiet or anxious, even the less assertive dog may think he needs to take charge. This is why it is very important to match pups to their owners very carefully and in particular avoid homing an assertive dog with a quiet, inexperienced handler. The dog might develop very successfully with stronger handling but without it, he may become difficult and challenging to live with.

Assertive behaviour is expressed in many different ways, which may include the following:

- Showing lack of respect for your personal space. For example, your dog will barge through doors ahead of you or jump up at you.
- Getting up on to the sofa or your favourite armchair and growling when you tell him to get back on the floor.
- Becoming possessive over a toy, or guarding his food bowl by growling when you get too close.
- Growling when anyone approaches his bed or when anyone gets too close to where he is lying.
- Ignoring basic obedience commands.
- Showing no respect to younger members of the family, pushing amongst them and completely ignoring them.
- Male dogs may start marking (cocking their leg) in the house.
- Aggression towards people (see page 100).

If you see signs of your Border

Collie becoming too assertive, you must work at lowering his status so that he realises that you are the leader and he must accept your authority. Although you need to be firm, you also need to use positive training methods so that your Border Collie is rewarded for the behaviour you want. In this way, his 'correct' behaviour will be strengthened and repeated.

There are a number of steps you can take to lower your Border Collie's status. They include:

- Go back to basics and hold daily training sessions. Make sure you have some really tasty treats, or find a toy your Border Collie really values and only bring it out at training sessions. Run through all the training exercises you have taught your Border Collie. Make a big fuss of him and reward him when he does well.

This will reinforce the message that you are the leader and that it is rewarding to do as you ask.

- Teach your Border Collie something new; this can be as simple as learning a trick, such as shaking paws. Having something new to think about will mentally stimulate your Border Collie and he will benefit from interacting with you.
- Be 100 per cent consistent with all house rules – your Border Collie must *never* sit on the sofa and you must *never* allow him to jump up at you.
- Make sure the family eats before you feed your Border Collie. Some trainers advocate eating in front of the dog (maybe just a few bites from a biscuit) before starting a training session, so the dog appreciates your elevated status.

If a dog has a weak leader he will seek to elevate his own status by breaking house rules.

TAKING CONTROL

Teaching the 'Leave' command correctly is really important, as it can be applied throughout your dog's life to avoid a wide variety of potentially dangerous situations. It is also a way of asserting your dominance over the dog, as it focuses on controlling access to his food.

- Command your dog to "Sit" and place his food bowl on the floor, giving the command "Leave". Initially you may have to restrain him by holding his collar.
- Wait a few seconds and then give a command, such as "OK" which releases the dog and allows him to go to the food bowl.
- Repeat this procedure at every mealtime. Soon your dog will learn to 'Leave' without being restrained. You can build up the amount of time your dog has to wait for the release to 5, 10 and then 15 seconds.
- Once 'Leave' has been learnt, playing with toys can have the dual value of positive interaction with your dog and asserting dominance by telling your dog to "Leave" or "Drop" the toy when you ask. Your Border Collie will see 'Drop' and 'Leave' as fun games and they are important in making sure it is clear who is the boss in the relationship.
- If your Border Collie is progressing well with his re-training programme, think about getting involved with a dog sport, such as Agility or competitive Obedience. This will give your Border Collie a positive outlet for his energies. However, if your Border Collie is still seeking to be dominant, or you have any other concerns, do not delay in seeking the help of an animal behaviourist.

- Do not let your Border Collie barge through doors ahead of you, or leap from the back of the car before you release him. You may need to put your dog on the lead and teach him to 'Wait' at doorways, and then reward him for letting you go through first.

AGGRESSION

Aggression is a complex issue, as there are different causes and the behaviour may be triggered by numerous factors. It may be directed towards people, but far more commonly it is directed towards other dogs.

Aggression in dogs may be the result of:

- Assertive behaviour (see page 98).
- Defensive behaviour: This may be induced by fear, pain or punishment.
- Territory: A dog may become aggressive if strange dogs or people enter his territory (which is generally seen as the house and garden).
- Intra-sexual issues: This is aggression between sexes – male to male or female to female.
- Parental instinct: A mother dog may become aggressive if she is protecting her puppies.

In order to learn social skills, it is important for a pup to stay with his mother until he is eight weeks of age. If a puppy has been inadequately socialised by leaving his mother too early and not having been socialised with other healthy older dogs, he will not learn 'dog language' which can result in communication problems with other dogs.

If the pup does not react appropriately to another dog in showing respect, by rolling over, keeping low and refraining from play behaviour when told to stop, he will be warned off by the older dog by growling. They may even take the pup by the neck and hold him to the ground. It is unlikely that a well-socialised older dog will ever harm a pup, but there are dogs that have left their mothers too early and have not learnt the necessary social skills.

A dog that experiences a negative interaction with other dogs, with the added negative reaction of the owner, will start to become very wary of other dogs and may decide to act defensively and even aggressively on a first strike basis rather than waiting for aggression from the other dog. Many dogs in the rescue system and in particular puppies from puppy farms show this tendency. Unfortunately, there is a danger that dog to dog aggression may then develop into dog to people aggression.

The impact upon a puppy of lack of contact with a 'mentor' dog in his early days is highly significant, and this has been shown in litters which have been deprived of their mother. The consequence is often that the puppies learn no dog language at all and are condemned to react inappropriately to other dogs. If a litter has to be hand reared through ill health or death of the mother, it is important to try to find another adult dog who will take them on as a foster parent to play this role.

It has been known for some experienced dog trainers to choose to collect their pups before eight weeks – even at six weeks old – to try to build a stronger relationship with their

The mother will teach lessons that will influence her puppies' outlook on life.

dog, in the belief it will help them with their later training. However, as a result the negative side effects can be seen later in life with dog to dog aggression as a recurring problem.

It is also important that bite inhibition is taught and your dog understands the need to have a soft mouth with people. This is another of the key things a puppy learns from his mother, littermates and potentially other adult dogs at the breeder. If the pup nips his mother in play he will be immediately corrected, but not hurt. Similarly, the pup will learn from his littermates that nipping results in cessation of play. Dog behaviourist Ian Dunbar describes learning bite inhibition as one of the crucial developmental stages that your dog needs to achieve if he is to be a well-socialised and 'safe' family pet.

One technique to teach this is to imitate the puppy's littermates, saying "Ouch" and turning away to stop play if the pup is ever anything other than gentle. On restarting play, it is

surprising how fast the pup demonstrates he has learnt that humans are very delicate and need to be handled with a very soft mouth.

Socialisation with people from an early age is very important to make sure that the dog will become a successful pack member with his future owner and will be confident with other people throughout his life. Puppies from puppy farms, or litters that have been reared in a barn that is distant from regular everyday view of people and regular interaction with people, will never fully recover from this. It will result in anxious and potentially aggressive dogs.

A Border Collie that has been well reared and bred from parents with a good temperament is very unlikely to develop dog to dog aggression or people aggression. However, any dog will respond to negative experiences in his life and the owner needs to take responsible action if any such thing happens and take advice on rehabilitating the dog.

Supervised play, including bite inhibition, is a vital part of a puppy's education.

CANINE SPORTS

If you enjoy training your Border Collie, you may want to try one of the many dog sports that are now on offer. The Border Collie will love every moment of his training and many will become highly successful in the chosen discipline.

SHEEPDOGS TRIALS

The Border Collie is still used as a working sheepdog, herding both sheep and cattle as well as helping with many tasks around the farm. A top working dog is highly prized, and the skills of both dog and handler can be tested at sheepdog trials. Sheepdog trials are organised by the International Sheepdog Society, which also registers some 6,000 Border Collie puppies every year. Many trials take place at a local level, organised by small groups, where all ages and abilities can compete. Nursery Trials are held for young dogs showing potential, and Open Trials are where handlers can gain points to permit entry to the National Trials. The National Trials for England, Ireland, Scotland and Wales are held every summer, along with the International (four nations) Trials. World Trials are staged every three years.

National Trials are run over a 400 yard (365 metre) course with five sheep, containing the standard elements of Outrun, Lift, Fetch, Drive, Shed, Pen, Single. The 15 highest placed competitors from each of the four National Trials meet together in competition at the International Trial.

At the International, the same size of course and number of sheep is used for the Qualifying Trial, which is run over the first two days, but on the third and final day, the highest placed 15 competitors, irrespective of country, meet to compete for the most coveted title in the sheepdog world – Supreme Champion. For this competition the course is lengthened to around 800 yards (732 metres), with the dog having to fetch one lot of sheep and then go back for a second. A total of 20 sheep are guided around the course. This is the greatest test any working sheepdog can possibly undertake. As far as possible, the conditions and work to be encountered in everyday shepherding on the hills and farms are followed at sheepdog trials.

Sheepdog Trials are very much the showcase of the working Border Collie, and the dogs that excel will be in demand for breeding so that their ability is passed on to future generations.

HERDING

Border Collies were bred to herd livestock and that instinct is still very strong in the modern Border Collie, even though it may be several generations since the dog actually worked sheep. Since 2007 the Border Collie Breed Council (BCBC) has been negotiating with the Kennel Club and the International Sheep Dog Society to modify the Working Test, in order that more Border Collies can take the test and become a full Champion instead of the limited Show Champion.

The Border Collie is the only breed in the KC's Pastoral Group that has to pass a herding test to become a full Champion. The Fédération Cynologique Internationale (FCI) also requires Border Collies to pass a herding test to become an International Champion. The Border Collie Breed Council have set up testing areas in the South, the Midlands and Scotland to encourage the herding capabilities of Border Collies.

The Working Test, which Show

Champion Border Collies must pass to gain promotion to the title of Champion, has now been replaced by a re-designed Herding Test. The new Herding Test aims to increase the number of Border Collies that achieve full Champion status. Like the original Working Test, which was introduced in 1992, the Herding Test is a limited version of a Sheepdog Trial. Its purpose is to safeguard the future development of the Border Collie by emphasising the importance of the breed's natural herding abilities.

The test consists of five principal elements: Outrun, Lift, Bring/Fetch, Inspection and Drive. The requirement to work sheep into a pen has been replaced by driving the sheep through a gate in the boundary of the test field. Distances have been reduced compared with the old Working Test and dogs are not required to lie down between the Outrun and the Lift sections. The time limit remains at 12 minutes. Dogs must now be at least 12 months old at the time of application for the test.

With the agreement of the International Sheep Dog Society, Herding Test judges will be appointed by the Kennel Club rather than from among ISDS Sheepdog Trial judges. Two judges will officiate at each trial, and the first three official judges approved by the Kennel Club are Marion Turner, Ann Jordan and Mike Conde, all of whom are active in showing Border Collies as well as in Sheepdog Trials.

Do you have ambitions to exhibit your Border Collie in the show ring?

SHOWING

In your eyes, your Border Collie is the most beautiful dog in the world – but would a judge agree? Showing is a highly competitive sport and the number entered in classes is increasing. However, many owners get bitten by the showing bug and their calendar is governed by the dates of the top showing fixtures.

To be successful in the show ring, a Border Collie must conform as closely as possible to the Breed Standard, which is a written blueprint describing the 'perfect' Border Collie (see Chapter Seven). To get started, you need to buy a puppy that has show potential and then train him to perform in the ring. A Border Collie will be expected to

stand in show pose, move around the ring for the judge in order to show off his natural gait, and to be examined by the judge. This involves a detailed hands-on examination, so your Border Collie must be bombproof when handled by strangers.

Many training clubs hold ringcraft classes, which are run by experienced show people. At these classes, you will learn how to handle your Border Collie in the ring and you will also find out about rules, procedures and show ring etiquette.

The best plan is to start off at some small, informal shows where you can practise and learn the tricks of the trade before graduating to bigger shows. It's a long haul starting in the very first puppy class, but the dream is to make your Border Collie up into a Show Champion.

COMPETITIVE OBEDIENCE

Border Collies dominate this sport, thriving on the precision and accuracy that the sport demands. The classes start off being relatively easy and become progressively more challenging, with additional exercises and the handler giving minimal instructions to the dog.

Exercises include:

- **Heelwork:** Dog and handler must complete a set pattern on and off the lead, which includes left turns, right turns, about turns and changes of pace.
- **Recall:** This may be when the handler is stationary or on the move.
- **Retrieve:** This may be a dumbbell or any article chosen by the judge.
- **Sendaway:** The dog is sent to a designated spot and must go into an instant 'Down' on command, until he is recalled by the handler.
- **Stays:** The dog must stay in the 'Sit' and in the 'Down' for a set amount of time. In advanced classes, the hander is out of sight,
- **Scent:** The dog must retrieve a single cloth from a pre-arranged pattern of cloths that

Picking up the correct cloth in a scent discrimination test is one of the harder exercises in Competitive Obedience.

has his owner's scent or, in advanced classes, the judge's scent. There may also be decoy cloths.

- **Distance control.** The dog must execute a series of moves (Sit, Stand, Down) without moving from his position and with the handler at a distance.

Many training clubs run advanced classes for those who want to compete in obedience, or you can hire the services of a professional trainer so you can have one-on-one sessions.

AGILITY

This fun sport has grown enormously in popularity over the past few years – and Border Collies excel at it. The only problem you have is curbing your dog's enthusiasm and gaining sufficient control to negotiate the complex courses at high speed.

In agility competitions, each dog must complete a set course over a series of obstacles, which include:

- Jumps (upright hurdles and long jump)
- Weaves
- A-frame
- Dog walk
- Seesaw
- Tunnels (collapsible and rigid)
- Tyre

Dogs may compete in 'Jumping' classes with jumps, tunnels and weaves, or in 'Agility' classes, which have the full set of equipment. Faults are awarded for poles down on the jumps, missed contact points on the A-frame, dog walk and seesaw, and refusals. If a dog takes the wrong course, he is eliminated. The winner is the dog that completes the course in the fastest time with no faults. As you progress up the levels, courses become progressively harder with more twists, turns and changes of direction.

If you want to get involved in Agility, you will need to find a club that specialises in the sport (see Appendices). You will not be allowed to start training until your Border Collie is 12 months old and you cannot compete until he is 18 months old. This rule is for the protection of the dog, who may suffer injury if he puts strain on bones and joints while he is still growing.

WORKING TRIALS

This is a very challenging sport, but the Border Collie, with his drive and initiative, can be very successful. The sport consists of three basic components:

- **Control:** Dog and handler must complete obedience exercises, but the work does not have to be as precise as it is in competitive obedience. In the advanced classes, 'manwork' (where the dog works as a guard/protection dog) is a major feature.
- **Agility:** The dog must negotiate a 3 ft (0.91 m) hurdle, a 9 ft (2.75 m) long jump and a 6 ft (1.82) upright scale, which is the most taxing piece of dog equipment.
- **Nosework:** The dog must follow a track that has been laid over a set course. The surface may vary, and the length of time between the track being laid and the dog starting work is increased in the advanced classes.

The ladder of stakes are: Companion Dog, Utility Dog, Working Dog, Tracking Dog and Patrol Dog. In the US, Tracking is a sport in its own right and is very popular among Border Collie owners.

If you want to get involved in Working Trials, you will need to find a specialist club or a trainer

The Border Collie is a fast and enthusiastic competitor in Agility.

that specialises in training for Working Trials. For more information, see Appendices.

FLYBALL

The Border Collie is fast and athletic and excels at this sport, which makes use of the chase and retrieve instincts. Flyball is a team sport; the dogs love it and it is undoubtedly the noisiest of all the canine sports!

Four dogs are selected to run in a relay race against an opposing team. The dogs are sent out by their handlers to jump four hurdles, catch the ball from the Flyball box and then return over the hurdles. At the top level, this sport is fast and furious and is dominated by Border Collies. In multibreed competitions, the team is made up of four dogs of different breeds and only one can be a Border Collie or a Working Sheepdog. Points are awarded to dogs and teams. Annual awards

are given to top dogs and top teams, and milestone awards are given out to dogs as they attain points throughout their Flyballing careers.

DANCING WITH DOGS

This sport is relatively new, but it is becoming increasingly popular. It is very entertaining to watch, but it is certainly not as simple as it looks. To perform a choreographed routine to music with your Border Collie demands a huge amount of training.

Dancing With Dogs is divided into two categories: Heelwork to Music and Canine Freestyle. In Heelwork to Music, the dog must work closely with his handler and show a variety of close 'heelwork' positions. In Canine Freestyle, the routine can be more flamboyant, with the dog working at a distance from the handler and performing spectacular tricks. Routines are judged on style and presentation, content and accuracy.

SUMMING UP

The Border Collie is the most versatile of all dogs: he is a tireless and highly skilled sheepdog, a fierce competitor in all the canine sports, and an outstanding companion. Make sure you keep your half of the bargain: spend time socialising and training your Border Collie so that you can be proud to take him anywhere and he will always be a credit to you.

THE PERFECT BORDER COLLIE

Chapter 7

Almost every owner of a Border Collie believes they have the ideal specimen, as beauty is so often in the eye of the beholder. For example, a lady came recently to look at puppies as her old Border Collie had died at the age of 15 years. She announced on arrival that she knew exactly what she was looking for, as her previous Border Collie was "perfect". Proudly, she showed me a picture of her beloved recently-departed dog. He was smooth coated with one ear up and one very heavy ear hanging down. The coat was predominantly white with some black splodges and he also had one blue eye. To this lady the dog was perfect and the way he looked at her in the picture, showed that he adored her as much as she adored him.

Obviously then, assessing the quality of a dog is a highly subjective issue, as some people value certain characteristics more than others. For this reason each breed of dog has a Breed Standard, which is a detailed description of the perfect specimen of the breed and it is against this ideal that dogs are judged at shows. A Breed Standard is effectively a blueprint of the perfect Border Collie and its existence helps to provide consistency and standardisation.

Breed Clubs and/or Breed Councils decide on the criteria which should be included in the Breed Standards, which are then ratified by the national kennel clubs.

The Kennel Club in Britain (KC), the American Kennel Club (AKC) and the Australian Kennel Club (AUS) all have different standards, as does the Federation Cynologique Internationale (FCI), which is based in Belgium and provides standards and show regulations for some 83 member countries. In fact, it is customary for the FCI standard to follow closely that of the country of origin, which in the case of the Border Collie, means the UK.

The standards are drawn up to assist judges, breeders and potential owners of Border Collies. It must be remembered that even though there are set criteria laid down, each person will interpret the standard slightly differently, which makes breeding and judging so interesting. Different interpretations of the standard are the reason why different dogs win at shows. Exhibitors will spend over £20 per entry and endure many hours of travel to experience the excitement of a different judge's opinion and interpretation of the Border Collie standard.

The extended version of the Australian Breed Standard is far more specific than the other standards, including the Australian

UK breed record holder Sh. Ch. Tonkory Palmerston at Fayken owned by Ross and Vicky Green

Am. Ch. Brackenhill Toncho Bon-Clyde: A typical American-bred Border Collie.

Multi Ch. Tonkory Incognito: A top winning dog in many European countries, including 2008 World Champion.

short version. It is a 27-page document with pictures and line drawings to illustrate the points made in the descriptions of the standard. Drawings of good and bad ear sets and eye shapes are very useful. Cow hocks or wide backends or forequarters are brought to life by the drawings.

It should be remembered that the kennel clubs only ratify the criteria decided upon by the Breed Clubs and/or Breed Councils. In the UK, the Kennel Club's Border Collie Breed Council acts as a consultative forum for the nine Border Collie Breed Clubs, which are listed in the appendix on page 147

Responding to public concern about the health of pure bred dogs, the KC has inserted the following introductory paragraph in all breed Standards:

A Breed Standard is the guideline which describes the ideal characteristics, temperament and appearance of a breed and ensures that the breed is fit for function. Absolute soundness is essential. Breeders and judges should at all times be careful to avoid obvious conditions or exaggerations which would be detrimental in any way to the health, welfare or soundness of this breed. From time to time certain conditions or exaggerations may be considered to have the potential to affect dogs in some breeds adversely, and judges and breeders are requested to refer to the Kennel Club website for details of any

The smooth outline of a Border Collie which should show gracefulness and perfect balance.

such current issues. If a feature or quality is desirable it should only be present in the right measure.

The following is my interpretation of the reasons behind each of the recommendations in the breed standard.

GENERAL APPEARANCE

KC & FCI
Well proportioned, smooth outline showing quality, gracefulness and perfect balance, combined with sufficient substance to give impression of endurance. Any tendency to coarseness or weediness undesirable.

AKC
The Border Collie is a well balanced, medium-sized dog of athletic appearance, displaying grace and agility in equal measure with substance and stamina. His hard, muscular body has a smooth outline which conveys the impression of effortless movement and endless endurance – characteristics which have made him the world's premier sheep herding dog. He is energetic, alert and eager. Intelligence is his hallmark.

AUS
The general appearance shall be that of a well proportioned dog, the smooth outline showing quality, gracefulness and perfect balance, combined with sufficient substance to ensure that it is capable of enduring long periods of active duty in its intended task as a working

109

The majority of Border Collies will have no contact with livestock, but the breed must retain the essential characteristics of a working sheepdog.

sheep dog. Any tendency to coarseness or weediness is undesirable.

All four standards stipulate balance, gracefulness, quality and sufficient substance. The dog must be balanced in order to work with stealth, agility and the ability to turn on a sixpence. There is nothing more graceful than a Border Collie, completely focused, working sheep. A dog that is too coarse or heavy loses the athleticism necessary to work and a weedy or insubstantial Border Collie would lack the strength, the stamina and the ability to hold strong sheep.

CHARACTERISTICS

KC & FCI
Tenacious, hardworking sheepdog, of great tractability.

AKC
See under General appearance above.

AUS
The Border Collie is highly intelligent, with an instinctive tendency to work and is readily responsive to training. Its

keen, alert and eager expression adds to its intelligent appearance, whilst its loyal and faithful nature demonstrates that it is at all times kindly disposed towards stock. Any aspect of structure or temperament foreign to a working dog is uncharacteristic.

The Border Collie was bred to herd and drive sheep and sometimes other stock on the farm. For this reason he must be fit, keen to work and able to keep going all day. Whether herding sheep in the Welsh or Scottish hills or the wide open spaces of New Zealand, Australia or America, he must have speed and strength for this arduous work. For these qualities to be judged in the show ring, the Border Collie must be able to gait tirelessly round the ring until the judge says 'stop' and for this reason the dog must be well-muscled and fit. The disadvantage for the handler is that he or she must also run round the ring, whereas if the dog is herding sheep the handler can sometimes remain in the area he wants the sheep brought to, i.e. the pen, or yard. In this respect, showing is

not always the soft option some people imagine!

TEMPERAMENT

KC & FCI
Keen, alert, responsive and intelligent. Neither nervous nor aggressive.

AKC
The Border Collie is intelligent, alert and responsive. Affectionate towards friends, he may be sensibly reserved towards strangers and therefore makes an excellent watchdog. An intensive worker while herding, he is eager to learn and to please, and thrives on human companionship. Any tendencies toward viciousness or extreme shyness are serious faults.

AUS
See under Characteristics above.

The farmer breeding Border Collies to work may not be concerned if the dog does not care to be with people, as that is not what he wants or needs from the dog. Most Border Collie breeders will however, sell the their puppies as pets, show dogs or for dog sports, so temperament is all important.

To show, the Border Collie must be steady when being examined by the judge, have his mouth opened for his teeth to be assessed and in the case of a male dog, be checked to ensure he has two fully descended testicles. He must also run around the ring with approximately 20 other dogs and settle on a bench for a good part of the day.

In obedience, the Border Collie must pass a temperament test to the satisfaction of the judge, must work without being distracted by other dogs and attend only to his handler. The Border Collie must also have the temperament to stand, sit and lie down in the proximity of other dogs without moving or interfering with them.

Living in a house with adults, children and other pets also requires a sound temperament, which in this case is of the utmost importance. Border Collies thrive on human companionship and they do become depressed or develop difficult traits if they are deprived of human contact. Their desire to be with people makes them supreme workmates.

HEAD AND SKULL

KC & FCI
Skull fairly broad, occiput not pronounced. Cheeks not full or rounded. Muzzle, tapering to nose, moderately short and strong. Skull and foreface

The Border Collie is a people orientated dog which means he can excel as workmate or purely as a companion.

approximately equal in length. Stop very distinct. Nose black, except in brown or chocolate colour when it may be brown. In blues nose should be slate colour. Nostrils well developed.

AKC
Expression is intelligent, alert, eager and full of interest. Eyes are set well apart, of moderate size, oval in shape. The color encompasses the full range of brown eyes; dogs having primary body colors other than black may have noticeably lighter eye color. Lack of eye rim pigmentation is a fault. Blue eyes are a fault except in merles, where one or both, or part of one or both eyes may be blue. Ears are of medium size, set well apart, carried erect and/or semi-erect (varying from $\frac{1}{4}$ to $\frac{3}{4}$ of the ear erect). The tips may fall forward or outward to the side. Ears are sensitive and mobile. Skull is broad with occiput not pronounced. Skull and foreface approximately equal in length. Stop moderate, but distinct. Muzzle moderately short, strong and blunt, tapering to nose. The underjaw is strong and well-developed. Nose color

The skull is broad, the muzzle is moderately short and strong, and the stop is very distinct.

matches the primary body color. Nostrils are well developed. A snipy muzzle is a fault. Bite: Teeth and jaws are strong, meeting in a scissors bite (ie: upper teeth closely overlapping lower teeth and set square to the jaws).

AUS
The skull is broad and flat between the ears, slightly narrowing to the eye, with a pronounced stop, cheeks deep but not prominent. The muzzle tapering to the nose, is strong and the same length as the skull. The lips are tight and clean and the nose is large with open nostrils. The nose colour in all dogs will be a solid colour with no pink or light pigment, and shall complement the background colour of the dog.

The Border Collie must have a fairly broad skull to accommodate the brain necessary to work sheep with his handler. The length of muzzle from the tip of the nose to the stop is equal to the length between the stop and the occiput. The head is balanced without exaggeration and the defined stop distinguishes the Border Collie from both the Rough or the Smooth Collie.

The Australian standard appears to tolerate more depth of cheek than the KC and FCI standards, which both require 'cheeks not full or rounded'.

The Border Collie must have a strong jaw to enable him to crunch bones and hold on to prey if necessary. I have observed two of my Border Collies pulling a rabbit apart after catching and

killing it. Like many other breeds, their jaws are incredibly strong and pet owners will often see them picking up a large log or hanging onto a 'tuggy' toy when playing.

The nostrils are required to be well developed and this is important for a breed such as the Border Collie that is very active and needs a free airway. It would be disastrous to attempt to change the shape of the head or nose in any way that would restrict the free flow of air to the lungs.

The AKC standard includes the eyes, ears and expression in the Head and Skull section whereas the KC, FCI and AUS standards describe them in separate sections.

EYES

KC & FCI
Set wide apart, oval shaped, of moderate size, brown in colour except in merles where one or both or part of one or both may be blue. Expression mild, keen, alert and intelligent.

AKC
See under Head and Skull above.

AUS
The eyes are set wide apart, oval shaped of moderate size harmonising with the colour of the coat but darker colour preferred, except in the case of chocolate where a lighter colour is permissible and in the case of merles where blue

The alert, intelligent expression that is so typical of the Border Collie.

A blue eye in a black and white Border Collie is considered a fault in the show ring – but it does not affect their sight.

is permissible. The expression is mild but keen, alert and intelligent.

All standards require that the eyes are set wide apart, in order to give the Border Collie good peripheral vision. The eyes should be oval shaped and of moderate size.

The American standard states that a range of brown eyes can be seen in Border Collies, whereas the KC and FCI just call for 'brown eyes'. The Australian standard states the eyes should harmonise with the coat colour but darker colour is preferred, except in the case of a chocolate coat, where a lighter eye is permissible. Merles can have one or both eyes blue, but blue with any other coat colour is a fault.

Over the years I have bred many litters of black and white Border Collies, and occasionally one puppy will have one blue eye. Although these dogs cannot be shown, it does not affect their sight and some prospective owners find it very appealing and special. The colour of the eye does affect the expression of the Border Collie. The darker eye gives a milder, kinder expression whereas a lighter, more yellow eye gives a harder expression.

Judges in the show ring will pay a lot of attention to the expression and alertness of the Border Collie and may test it by throwing something in front of the dog to see if it responds.

If you watch a Border Collie working sheep, you will see his expression change the minute he

sees them. He is immediately alert and his every sense comes into play.

The shape of the eye is also important. A Border Collie with too small an eye can look mean, whereas a round eye can look too starey.

EARS

KC & FCI
Medium sized and texture, well set apart. Carried erect or semi-erect and sensitive in use.

AKC
See under Head and Skull above.

AUS
The ears should be of medium size and texture, set well apart,

EAR CARRIAGE

The ears are set well apart and most be used with sensitivity. This Border Collie has semi-erect ears.

This Border Collie has erect ears, which is acceptable in all Breed Standards, with the exception of the Australian version.

carried semi-erect. They are sensitive in their use, and inside well furnished with hair.

Only the Australian standard requires semi-erect ears, which are furnished on the inside with hair, whereas the KC, FCI and AKC standards accept erect as well as semi-erect ears in the Border Collie. All the standards however, require the ears to be sensitive in use.

Border Collies are extremely sound sensitive. They need this acute sense of hearing to detect a lost lamb as well as to listen to the distant commands of the shepherd or obedience handler. This characteristic is also useful in search and rescue. To accommodate this sound sensitivity, the ear is appropriately shaped.

In the show ring, the shape and use of the ears adds to the Border Collie's expression, but judges vary in their attention to this characteristic. There is no doubt that a dog with up and tipped ears who is looking attentively at whatever is going on around him, is more attractive than a drop-eared dog that looks disinterested. This however, should never be seen as more important than the conformation and movement of the Border Collie.

I have an old Border Collie bitch, a past top brood bitch, who is now diabetic and partially blind. As her sight deteriorates, her ears come up higher and higher as she is listening more intently rather than watching.

Some breeders routinely test puppies for hearing as both bilateral and unilateral deafness can occur on occasions and only scientific testing can detect and confirm this. The Animal Health Trust in Cambridge has the equipment and specialists to carry out these tests.

MOUTH

KC & FCI
Teeth and jaws strong with a perfect, regular and complete scissor bite.

AKC
See under Head and Skull above.

AUS
The teeth should be sound, strong and evenly spaced, the lower incisors just behind but touching the upper, that is a scissor bite.

The perfect scissor bite is required in all the standards. Mouths that are overshot (upper jaw protruding in front of lower jaw) or undershot (lower jaw protruding in front of upper jaw) are faults and will be penalised in the show ring. A level bite is also a fault.

None of the standards stipulate the number of teeth, but the Border Collie should have 42 – 20 in the upper jaw and 22 in the lower jaw. There should be 6 incisors, 2 canines and 8 premolars in both the upper and lower jaws and 4 and 6 molars in the upper and lower jaws respectively. The teeth should all be clean.

In the UK, USA and Australia, judges very rarely count teeth but in Europe, particularly Germany, judges count premolars and penalise for missing teeth. It is important that exhibitors know this, as with the Pet Passport Scheme more and more British Border Collie owners are showing their dogs elsewhere in Europe.

If an accident or infection occurs and extraction of teeth is necessary, then the owner must have a vet's letter of explanation and permission from the Kennel

The teeth should meet in a scissor bite with the teeth on the upper jaw closely overlapping the teeth on the lower jaw.

Club, to continue to show the dog. In the UK, Challenge Certificates have been awarded to Border Collies with missing teeth, but the judge needs to be certain the teeth were there originally.

NECK

KC
Of good length, strong and muscular, slightly arched and broadening to shoulders.

FCI
Of good length, strong and muscular, slightly arched and broadening to shoulders. Topline is level, with slight arch over the loins. Body is athletic in appearance.

USA
Neck is of good length, strong and muscular, slightly arched and broadening to shoulders. Topline is level, with slight arch over the loins. Body is athletic in appearance. Chest is deep, moderately broad, showing great lung capacity. Brisket reaching to the point of the elbow. Rib cage well sprung. Loins moderately deep, muscular, slightly arched with no tuck-up. Croup gradually sloped downward.

AUS
The neck is of good length, strong and muscular, slightly arched and broadening to the shoulders, without throatiness or coarseness.

The neck needs to be strong and muscled to support the head, particularly when eyeing or holding the sheep. The neck will be extended in the characteristic crouching position, with the nose, head and body almost level, as we have all seen in 'One Man And His Dog'. The neck also needs to be of good length to enable the dog to see into the distance and over long grass or rough terrain.

The Australian standard states there should be no throatiness or coarseness. In the show ring, a Border Collie with a short or 'stuffy' neck lacks elegance and balance. The judge must check the length with his hands, as sometimes an abundance of coat can make the neck look short.

The fore legs are well boned, and parallel when viewed from the front.

FOREQUARTERS

KC & FCI

Front legs parallel when viewed from front, pasterns slightly sloping when viewed from side. Bone strong, but not heavy. Shoulders well laid back, elbows close to body.

AKC

Forelegs well-boned and parallel when viewed from front, pasterns slightly sloping when viewed from side. The shoulders are long and well-angulated to the upper arm. The elbows are neither in nor out. Dewclaws may be removed. Feet are compact, oval in shape, pads deep and strong, toes moderately arched and close together.

AUS

The shoulders are long, and well angulated to the upper arm, neither in nor out at elbow. The forelegs are well boned, straight and parallel when viewed from the front. Pasterns show flexibility with a slight slope when viewed from the side.

The American standard says that dewclaws may be removed, but in 30 years of judging and showing in Britain and Europe, I have never seen a Border Collie with the front dewclaws removed.

All standards agree that the shoulders should be well laid. This means the shoulder blade or scapula should be a good length, although nowhere is it stipulated exactly what length it should be. For Border Collies, the shoulder blade should meet the upper arm at an angle of 90 degrees and this, with the correct length of shoulder, ensures that the dog can move with good extension of the front legs from minimum lift.

There is growing concern among judges in Britain that breeders are not producing Border Collies with well angulated shoulders and upper arms and therefore, they do not have the characteristic or desired front movement. A good judge will feel for the length of shoulder and the angle to the upper arm. The correctness of proportions is then usually confirmed when you watch the dog move across the ring and certainly, when it is asked to gait round the ring. Steep shoulders with a lack of correct angulation produce a hackneyed or stiff, rather stilted movement.

The elbows should be close in to the body. If the elbows are out, then the front legs appear slightly bowed and the dog 'toes in' in at the front. This fault can be easily seen as the dog is moved across the ring towards the judge.

The pasterns should show flexibility, with a slight slope when viewed from the side. The pasterns are the shock absorbers and need to be flexible to allow the Border Collie to work over uneven ground.

I would watch my Border Collie negotiate a rocky coastline with the utmost agility while walking on holiday. If a prospective owner wants a companion to accompany him on a walking holiday, a Border Collie is admirably suited for this.

BODY

KC & FCI

Athletic in appearance, ribs well sprung, chest deep and rather broad, loins deep and muscular, but not tucked up. Body slightly longer than height at shoulder.

AKC

Body is athletic in appearance. Chest is deep, moderately broad, showing great lung capacity. Brisket reaching to the point of the elbow. Rib cage well sprung. Loins moderately deep, muscular, slightly arched with no tuck-up. Croup gradually sloped downward.

AUS

The body is moderately long with well sprung ribs tapering to a fairly deep and moderately broad chest. The loins are broad, deep, muscular and only slightly arched, flanks deep and not cut up.

The body is slightly longer than the height at the shoulder.

The body should be slightly longer than the height at the shoulder and athletic in appearance. The UK, FCI and American standards all stipulate athleticism and it is interesting to note there is much discussion in the UK about the loss of athletic appearance as glamour takes preference among some Border Collie breeders.

The American standard is the only one to mention the topline of a Border Collie, which should be level with a slight rise over the loin, although in other countries judges usually penalise weak or 'dippy' toplines.

All the standards agree that the chest should be well ribbed and deep. This is to accommodate the heart and lungs necessary to achieve the required endurance in a Border Collie. There is also agreement that the loins should be rather broad, deep and muscular but not tucked up.

HINDQUARTERS

KC & FCI

Broad, muscular, in profile sloping gracefully to set on of tail. Thighs long, deep and muscular with well turned stifles and strong, well let down hocks. From hock to ground, hindlegs well boned and parallel when viewed from rear.

AKC

Broad and muscular, in profile sloping gracefully to set of tail. The thighs are long, broad, deep and muscular, with well-turned stifles and strong hocks, well let down. When viewed from the rear, hind legs are well-boned, straight and parallel or are very slightly cow-hocked.

The powerful hindquarters provide drive from behind.

AUS

The hindquarters are broad and muscular, in profile sloping gracefully to the set on of tail. The thighs are long, broad, deep and muscular with well

turned stifles and strong hocks, well let down, and when viewed from the rear are straight and parallel.

The hindquarters form the powerhouse of the Border Collie, providing the essential drive. This part of the dog is so important that there appears to be agreement on the requirements in most of the standards.

Although Border Collies move closer behind than some other breeds, there is no excuse for a 'knitting' hind action or rubbing of hocks. The USA standard says the hind legs when viewed from behind should be 'well-boned straight and parallel or are very slightly cow-hocked'. I would certainly not agree with this and I view cow-hocks as a weakness. This is so obvious when such dogs try to move at a trot or a gallop.

The slope of the croup is important and some Border Collies look very square, lacking gracefulness. Hind angulation is quite a problem in some Border Collies, with the tibia having insufficient length and the hocks being too long. Some stifles are very straight and lacking angulation. The dog is, therefore, not capable of driving forward.

FEET

KC & FCI

Oval in shape, pads deep, strong and sound, toes arched and close together. Nails short and strong.

AKC

Dewclaws may be removed. Feet are compact, oval in shape, pads deep and strong, toes moderately arched and close together. Nails are short and strong.

AUS

Oval in shape, pads deep, strong and sound, toes moderately arched and close together. Nails short and strong.

The feet of the Border Collie are very important, as they carry the weight of a dog which must be able to cover vast areas of rough ground at speed. The muscled tightness of the feet is, therefore, imperative and the paws must be well padded for protection. Some show judges will pick up the feet and examine them.

Hind dewclaws are not required in Border Collies and the American standard states that they may be removed. This is not stated in the UK, FCI and Australian standards, but most breeders have the hind dewclaws removed by the vet when puppies are a day old, if they are present.

TAIL

KC & FCI

Moderately long, the bone reaching at least to hock, set on low, well furnished and with an upward swirl towards the end, completing graceful contour and balance of dog. Tail may be raised in excitement, never carried over back.

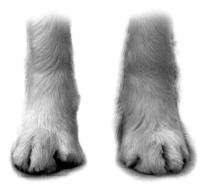

The feet are oval in shape with arched toes.

AKC

Tail is set low. It is moderately long, bone reaching at least to the hock. It may have an upward swirl to the tip. While concentrating at a given task, the tail is carried low and used for balance. In excitement it may rise level with the back. A gay tail is a fault.

AUS

The tail is moderately long, set on low, well furnished and with an upward swirl towards the end, completing the graceful contour and balance of the dog. The tail may be raised in excitement, but not carried over the back.

It is sometimes said that the brains of a Border Collie are in his tail, a result of the fact that when he is working and concentrating his tail is held low. It is certainly the rudder of the dog and is used for balancing when he is twisting and turning, whether herding or doing sports such as Agility or Flyball.

The Border Collie must be trained to carry his tail low in the show ring, as he is not concentrating in the same way as when he herding sheep. Dogs in the show ring are often excited and allow their tails to 'fly'. This completely spoils the balance of the dog and the outline and grace is destroyed.

A long, well-set and low-carried tail certainly completes the picture of the archetypal Border Collie.

GAIT/MOVEMENT

KC & FCI

Free, smooth and tireless, with minimum lift of feet, conveying impression of ability to move with great stealth and speed.

AKC

The Border Collie is an agile dog, able to suddenly change speed and direction without loss of balance and grace. Endurance is his trademark. His trotting gait is free, smooth and tireless, with minimum lift of feet. The topline does not shift as he conveys an effortless glide. He moves with great stealth, strength and stamina. When viewed from the side, the stride should cover maximum ground, with minimum speed. Viewed from the front, the action is forward and true, without weakness in shoulders, elbows or pasterns. Viewed from behind, the quarters

The Border Collie must carry his tail low to show that he is working.

A moderately long coat, with abundant feathering.

thrust with drive and flexibility, with hocks moving close together but never touching. Any deviation from a sound-moving dog is a fault. In final assessment, gait is an essential factor, confirming physical evaluation.

AUS

The movement is free, smooth and tireless, with a minimum lift of the feet, conveying the impression of the ability to move with great stealth. The action, viewed from the front, should be straight forward and true, without weakness at shoulders, elbows or pasterns. Viewed from behind the quarters thrust with strength and flexibility, with hocks not close nor too far apart. When trotting, the dog's feet tend to come closer together as speed increases, but when the dog comes to rest he should stand four square. Any tendency to stiltedness or to cow hocks or bow hocks is a serious fault.

The UK and FCI standards are fairly succinct and self explicit about the movement of the Border Collie, whereas the American and Australian standards are more detailed in their description of movement. These also include descriptions of front and hind movement.

As a championship show judge, movement of the Border Collie is of paramount importance to me. I do like to see soundness when the dog is coming towards me and going away, and a smooth flowing gait round the ring. This to me confirms the good conformation of the dog. Many dogs on the stand look glorious when stacked up but disappoint when on the move.

The smooth-coated Border Collie is often favoured as a working dog, but the heavier coat is preferred in the show ring.

COAT

KC & FCI

Two varieties: 1) Moderately long; 2) Smooth. In both, topcoat dense and medium textured, undercoat soft and dense giving good weather resistance. In moderately long coated variety, abundant coat forms mane, breeching and brush. On face, ears, forelegs (except for feather), hindlegs from hock to ground, hair should be short and smooth.

AKC

Two varieties are permissible, both having soft, dense, weather resistant double coat. In puppies, the coat is short, soft, dense and water resistant, becoming the undercoat in adult dogs. The rough coat is medium to long, texture from flat to slightly wavy. Short and smooth coat on face. Forelegs feathered. Rear pasterns may have coat trimmed short. With advancing age, coats may become very wavy and are not faulted. The smooth coat is short over entire body. May have feathering on forelegs and fuller coat on chest.

AUS

Double coated, with a moderately long, dense, medium textured topcoat while the undercoat is short, soft and dense, making a weather resisting protection, with abundant coat to form mane, breeching and brush. On face, ear tips, forelegs (except for feather), hind legs from hock to ground, the hair is short and smooth.

The Border Collie needs a good double coat to protect him from the driving rain and wind as well as the low temperatures he is

Colours such as merles and sables are judged equally with dogs that have more traditional markings.

and feet of the Border Collie to tidy them up and American exhibitors put more emphasis on grooming and presenting their dogs than is usual in the UK and Europe. This difference is changing as the Border Collie continues to gain popularity in the UK and Europe as a show dog. This in itself is a controversial point, as some enthusiasts do not want the Border Collie to become a show dog to the detriment of his working ability.

COLOUR

KC & FCI
Variety of colours permissible. White should never predominate.

AKC
The Border Collie appears in many colors, with various combinations of patterns and markings. The most common color is black with or without the traditional white blaze, collar, stockings and tail tip, with or without tan points. However, a variety of primary body colors is permissible. The sole exception being all white. Solid color, bi-color, tri-color, merle and sable dogs are judged equally with dogs having traditional markings. Color and markings are always secondary to physical evaluation and gait.

AUS
Black and white, blue and white, chocolate and white, red

likely to encounter while working sheep in the hills. Some shepherds prefer a smooth coated Border Collie, as the coat is easier to manage and does not get tangled in briars and other thick undergrowth.

For the show ring a heavier coat is preferred and when well groomed this can look very glamorous. But it is to be hoped that Border Collies are not bred to carry as much coat as Rough

Collies, as this would be very wrong.

The Border Collie Club of Great Britain used to put on classes for smooth coated Border Collies at their shows and I can remember some beautiful, shapely and sound specimens being shown. These classes, however, ceased to attract many entries and were eventually discontinued.

Exhibitors do trim the hocks

and white, blue merle and the tri-colour black, tan and white. In each case the basic body colour must predominate and be the background colour of the dog.

The American and Australian standards are far more specific than the UK and FCI standards, as they both name acceptable colours.

The Border Collie Breed Council did discuss the issue of colour some years ago when some people bred colours such as lilac and white, claiming they were rare and therefore, more valuable. After much discussion it was decided to leave the standard unchanged.

Shepherds do not favour white dogs as they can be difficult to see among the sheep and it is believed that the sheep do not respect a white dog.

SIZE

UK & FCI
Ideal height: Dogs 53 cms (21 ins); Bitches slightly less.

AKC
The height at the withers varies from 19 inches to 22 inches for males, 18 to 21 for females. The body, from point of shoulder to buttocks, is slightly longer than the height at the shoulders. Bone must be strong, not excessive, always in proportion to size. Overall balance between height, length, weight and bone is crucial and is more important than any

The Border Collie should not err too far from the correct height, but balance and proportion are equally important considerations.

absolute measurement. Excess body weight is not to be mistaken for muscle or substance. Any single feature of size appearing out of proportion should be considered a fault

AUS
Height: Dogs 48-53 cm (approx. 19-21 ins) at withers. Bitches 46-51 cm (approx. 18-20 ins) at withers.

Most of the standards recommend heights of approximately 21 inches for males and 19 inches for females, although the American and Australian standards give a little more specific leeway.

Shepherds use dogs of varying sizes, some a little above the standard and some below, as long as they can carry out the job required of them.

In the show ring, I think over

The top priority is to produce a sound, healthy dog that is still capable of carrying out a day's work in harsh conditions.

the last 30 years the Border Collie has probably become slightly smaller, although there are still some top sized dogs being shown. The most important thing is that the dog is balanced and in proportion, even if he is slightly outside the standard.

FAULTS

KC & FCI
Any departure from the foregoing points should be considered a fault and the seriousness with which the fault should be regarded be in exact proportion to its degree.

AKC
Any deviation from the foregoing should be considered a fault, the seriousness of the fault depending upon the extent of the deviation.

AUS
Any departure from the foregoing points should be considered a fault and the seriousness with which the fault should be regarded should be in exact proportion to its degree.

All the standards are in agreement about faults. Some obedience exhibitors will ignore structural faults if they do not interfere with the precision of working. Of course, coat and eye colour are of no consequence at all if the Border Collie is sufficiently switched on and willing to work.

NOTE

Male animals should have two apparently normal testicles fully descended into the scrotum.

Although there is no mention in the American standard about males having two fully descended testicles, the dog would be disqualified under AKC rules if it was missing a testicle.

I certainly have experienced judging Minor Puppy and Puppy classes where there has been an undescended testicle and this applies to many breeds. In some breeds it can take up to a year for both testicles to fully descend and the judge must decide whether to penalise or not depending on the quality overall.

There is growing controversy in the UK about whether the Border Collie is being developed as a glamorous show dog and losing its original characteristics and there has always been a section of the American Border Collie enthusiasts that have maintained a more working type of Border Collie. Whilst visiting a Specialty show in Louiseville, USA, I noticed a few entries from the more working type supporters of the Border Collie. These dogs were distinctly different – generally smaller, with less coat and bone and some had pricked ears. They seemed to represent the extremity of difference in working and show Border Collies. I make this observation based on seeing some very handsome, strong, heavy-coated dogs working in ISDS Sheepdog Trials.

A BBC television documentary in 2008 about pedigree dogs, highlighted the dangers of man interfering too much with the appearance of several breeds. The general accusation was that breeders are producing unhealthy dogs with inherent faults in the service of fashion.

Fortunately I think the Border Collie has been changed comparatively little from its origin, mainly because it has been bred to do the job it was intended for. When the Border Collie was being bred entirely to herd and work stock, it was closely scrutinised and if it did not do the job it was supposed to do, it was disposed of and certainly never used for breeding. Early pedigrees show some very close matings and in some cases these worked well. We will probably never know the close matings that produced faults.

The good news is that Border Collie owners through the Breed Clubs and Breed Councils have put enormous amounts of time and effort into raising money to sponsor research into hereditary diseases such as CEA, TNS, CL and we are currently looking at cancer, epilepsy and monorchidism. We now have the benefit of DNA testing for Collie Eye Anomaly (CEA), Trapped Neutrophil Syndrome (TNS) and Ceriod Lipofuscinosis (CL) for both affected dogs and defective gene carriers and with this knowledge, we can hopefully breed out all of these three hereditary diseases from Border Collies (see Chapter 8: Happy and Healthy.).

HAPPY AND HEALTHY

The Border Collie is a resilient dog, active in mind and body. He was developed as a working dog and should enjoy a life-span running well into double figures provided his needs are met. He is as well suited to being trained to work sheep, living outside on a farm, as he is to living indoors as a loyal member of the family, showing off his intelligence in the obedience ring.

The Border Collie is renowned as a plucky, faithful companion and a willing friend on a non-conditional basis. He will however, of necessity rely on you for food and shelter, accident prevention and medication. He also needs to be kept occupied mentally – a bored Border Collie is to be avoided at all costs! A healthy Border Collie is a tail-wagging happy dog, seeking only to please his owner. Many will

spontaneously hunt out an item such as a favourite ball or a slipper to give to their owner when he or she walks in the door, as a way of saying 'Welcome home!'

There are a few genetic conditions which occur in the Border Collie, which will be covered in depth later in the chapter.

ROUTINE HEALTH CARE

VACCINATION

There is much debate over the issue of vaccination at the moment. The timing of the final part of the initial vaccination course for a puppy and the frequency of subsequent booster vaccinations are both under scrutiny. An evaluation of the relative risk for each disease plays a part, depending on the local situation.

Many owners think that the actual vaccination is the protection, so that their puppy can go out for walks as soon as he or she has had the final part of the puppy vaccination course. This is not the case. The rationale behind vaccination is to stimulate the immune system into producing protective antibodies, which will be triggered if the patient is subsequently exposed to that particular disease. This means that a further one or two weeks will have to pass before an effective level of protection will have developed.

Vaccines against viruses stimulate longer-lasting protection than those against bacteria, whose effect may only persist for a matter of months in some cases. There is also the possibility of an individual failing to mount a full immune response to a vaccination:

The booster vaccination gives an opportunity for your dog to have a thorough health check.

although the vaccine schedule may have been followed as recommended, that particular dog remains vulnerable.

A dog's level of protection against rabies, as demonstrated by the antibody titre in a blood sample, is routinely tested in the UK in order to fulfil the requirements of the Pet Travel Scheme (PETS). This is not required at the current time with any other individual diseases in order to gauge the need for booster vaccination or to determine the effect of a course of vaccines; instead, your veterinary surgeon will advise a protocol based upon the vaccines available, local disease prevalence and the lifestyle of you and your dog.

It is worth remembering that maintaining a fully effective level of immune protection against the diseases appropriate to your locale is vital: these are serious diseases, which may result in the death of your dog, and some may have the potential to be passed on to his human family (so-called zoonotic potential for transmission). This is where you will be grateful for your veterinary surgeon's own knowledge and advice.

The American Animal Hospital Association laid down guidance at the end of 2006 for the

Kennel cough spreads rapidly among dogs that live together.

vaccination of dogs in North America. Core diseases were defined as distemper, adenovirus, parvovirus and rabies. So-called non-core diseases are kennel cough, Lyme disease and leptospirosis. A decision to vaccinate against one or more non-core diseases will be based on an individual's level of risk, determined on lifestyle and where you live in the United States.

Do remember however, that the booster visit to the veterinary surgery is not 'just' for a booster. I am regularly correcting my clients when they announce that they have 'just' brought their pet for a booster. Instead, this appointment is a chance for a full health check and evaluation of how a particular dog is doing. After all, we are all conversant with the adage that a human year is equivalent to seven canine years.

There have been attempts in recent times to reset the scale for two reasons: small breeds live longer than giant breeds, and dogs are living longer than previously. I have seen dogs of 17 and 18 years of age, but to say a dog is 119 or 126 years old is plainly meaningless. It does emphasise the fact though, that a dog's health can change dramatically over the course of a single year, because dogs age at a far faster rate than humans.

For me as a veterinary surgeon, the booster vaccination visit is a challenge: how much can I find of which the owner was unaware, such as rotten teeth or a heart murmur? Even monitoring bodyweight year upon year is of use, because bodyweight can creep up or down, without an owner realising. Being overweight

is unhealthy, but it may take an outsider's remark to make an owner realise that there is a problem. Conversely, a drop in bodyweight may be the only pointer to an underlying problem.

The diseases against which dogs are vaccinated include:

ADENOVIRUS
Canine adenovirus 1 (CAV-1) affects the liver (hepatitis) and is seen within affected dogs as the classic 'blue eye', while CAV-2 is a cause of kennel cough (see later). Vaccines often include both canine adenoviruses.

DISTEMPER
This disease is sometimes called 'hardpad' from the characteristic changes to the pads of the paws. It has a worldwide distribution, but fortunately vaccination has

LEPTOSPIROSIS

This disease is caused by *Leptospira interogans*, a spiral-shaped bacterium. There are several natural variants or serovars. Each is characteristically found in one or more particular host animal species, which then acts as a reservoir, intermittently shedding leptospires in the urine. Infection can also be picked up at mating, via bite wounds, across the placenta, or through eating the carcases of infected animals (such as rats).

A serovar will cause actual clinical disease in an individual when two conditions are fulfilled: the individual is not the natural host species, and is also not immune to that particular serovar.

Leptospirosis is a zoonotic disease, known as Weil's disease in humans, with implications for all those in contact with an affected dog. It is also commonly called 'rat jaundice', reflecting the rat's important role as a carrier. The UK National Rodent Survey 2003 found a wild brown rat population of 60 million, equivalent at the time to one rat per person. Wherever you live in the UK, rats are endemic, which means that the Border Collie living with a family in a town, is as much at risk as the Border Collie leading a rural lifestyle working with sheep and cattle in the countryside.

Signs of illness reflect the organs affected by a particular serovar. In humans, there may be a flu-like illness or a more serious, often life-threatening disorder involving major body organs. The illness in a susceptible dog may be mild, the dog recovering within two to three weeks without treatment but going on to develop long-term liver or kidney disease. In contrast, peracute illness may result in a rapid deterioration and death following an initial malaise and fever. There may also be anorexia, vomiting, diarrhoea, abdominal pain, joint pain, increased thirst and urination rate, jaundice and ocular changes. Haemorrhage is also a common feature, manifesting as bleeding under the skin, nosebleeds and the presence of blood in the urine and faeces.

Treatment requires rigorous intravenous fluid therapy to support the kidneys. Being a bacterial infection, it is possible to treat leptospirosis with specific antibiotics, although a prolonged course of several weeks is needed. Strict hygiene and barrier nursing are required in order to avoid onward transmission of the disease.

Vaccination reduces the severity of disease, but cannot prevent the dog becoming a carrier.

The situation in America is less clear-cut. Blanket vaccination against leptospirosis is not considered necessary, because it only occurs in certain areas. There has also been a shift in the serovars implicated in clinical disease, reflecting the effectiveness of vaccination and the migration of wildlife reservoirs carrying different serovars from rural areas, so you must be guided by your veterinarian's knowledge of the local situation.

been very effective at reducing its occurrence. It is caused by a virus and affects the respiratory, gastro-intestinal (gut) and nervous systems, so it causes a wide range of illnesses. Fox and urban stray dog populations are most at risk and are usually responsible for local outbreaks.

KENNEL COUGH
Also known as **infectious tracheobronchitis**, *Bordetella bronchiseptica* is not only a major cause of kennel cough, but also a common secondary infection on top of another cause. Being a bacterium, it is susceptible to treatment with appropriate antibiotics, but the immunity stimulated by the vaccine is

Fortunately, Lyme disease is relatively rare in the UK.

therefore short-lived (six to 12 months).

This vaccine is often in a form to be administered down the nostrils in order to stimulate local immunity at the point of entry, so to speak. Do not be alarmed to see your veterinary surgeon using a needle and syringe to draw up the vaccine, because the needle will be replaced with a special plastic introducer, allowing the vaccine to be gently instilled into each nostril. Dogs generally resent being held, more than the actual intra-nasal vaccine and I have learnt that covering the patient's eyes helps greatly.

Kennel cough is, however, rather a catch-all term for any cough spreading within a dog population – not just in kennels, but also between dogs at a training session or breed show, or even mixing in the park. Many of these infections may not be *B. bronchiseptica* but other viruses, for which one can only treat symptomatically.

Parainfluenza virus is often included in a vaccine programme, as it is a common viral cause of kennel cough.

Kennel cough can seem alarming. There is a persistent cough accompanied by the production of white frothy spittle, which can last for a matter of weeks; during this time the patient is highly infectious to other dogs. I remember when it ran through our five Border Collies – there were white patches of froth on the floor wherever you looked! Other features include sneezing, a runny nose and eyes sore with conjunctivitis. Fortunately, these infections are generally self-limiting, most dogs recovering without any long-lasting problems, but an elderly dog may be knocked sideways by it, akin to the effects of a common cold on a frail, elderly person.

LYME DISEASE
This is a bacterial infection transmitted by hard ticks. It is

RABIES

This is another zoonotic disease and there are very strict control measures in place. Vaccines were once available in the UK only on an individual basis for dogs being taken abroad. Pets travelling into the UK had to serve six months compulsory quarantine, so that any pet incubating rabies would be identified before release back into the general population. Under the Pet Travel Scheme (PETS), provided certain criteria are met (check the DEFRA website for up to date information – www.defra.gov.uk), then dogs can re-enter the UK without being quarantined.

Dogs to be imported into the United States have to show that they were vaccinated against rabies at least 30 days previously; otherwise, they have to serve effective internal quarantine for 30 days from the date of vaccination against rabies, in order to ensure they are not incubating the disease. The exception are dogs entering from countries recognised as being rabies-free, in which case it has to be proved that they lived in that country for at least six months beforehand.

restricted to those specific areas of the United States where ticks are found, such as the north-eastern states, some southern states, California and the upper Mississippi region. It does also occur in the UK, but at a low level, so vaccination is not routinely offered.

Clinical disease is manifested primarily as limping due to arthritis, but other organs affected include the heart, kidneys and nervous system. It is readily treatable with appropriate antibiotics, once diagnosed, but the causal bacterium *Borrelia burgdorferi* is not cleared from the body totally and will persist.

Prevention requires both vaccination and tick control, especially as there are other diseases transmitted by ticks. Ticks carrying *B. burgdorferi* will transmit it to humans as well, but an infected dog cannot pass it to a human.

PARVOVIRUS (CPV)

Canine parvovirus disease first appeared in the late 1970s, when it was feared that the UK's dog population would be decimated by it because of the lack of immunity in the general canine population. While this was a terrifying possibility at the time, fortunately it did not happen.

There are two forms of the virus (CPV-1, CPV-2) affecting domesticated dogs. It is highly contagious, picked up via the mouth/nose from infected faeces. The incubation period is about five days. CPV-2 causes two types of illness: gastro-enteritis and heart disease in puppies born to unvaccinated dams, both of which often result in death. Infection of puppies under three weeks of age with CPV-1 manifests as diarrhoea, vomiting, difficulty breathing and fading puppy syndrome. CPV-1 can cause abortion and foetal abnormalities in breeding bitches.

Occurrence is mainly low now, thanks to vaccination, although a recent outbreak in my area did claim the lives of several puppies and dogs. It is also occasionally seen in the elderly unvaccinated dog.

PARASITES

A parasite is defined as an organism deriving benefit on a one-way basis from another, the host. It goes without saying that it is not to the parasite's advantage to harm the host to such an extent that the benefit is lost, especially if it results in the death of the host. This means a dog could harbour parasites, internal and/or external, without there being any signs apparent to the owner. Many canine parasites can, however, transfer to humans with variable consequences, so routine preventative treatment is advised against particular parasites.

Just as with vaccination, risk assessment plays a part – for example, there is no need for routine heartworm treatment in the UK (at present), but it is vital in the United States and in Mediterranean countries.

ROUNDWORMS (NEMATODES)

These are the spaghetti-like worms that you may have seen passed in faeces or brought up in vomit. Most of the de-worming treatments in use today cause the adults roundworms to disintegrate, thankfully, so that treating puppies in particular is not as unpleasant as it used to be!

Most puppies will have a worm burden, mainly of a particular roundworm species (*Toxocara canis*), which reactivates within the dam's tissues during pregnancy and passes to the foetuses developing in the womb. It is therefore important to treat the dam both during and after pregnancy, as well as the puppies.

Professional advice is to continue worming every one to three months. There are roundworm eggs in the environment and unless you examine your dog's faeces under a microscope on a very regular basis for the presence of roundworm eggs, you will be unaware of your dog having picked up roundworms, unless he should have such a heavy burden that he passes the adults.

It takes a few weeks from the time that a dog swallows a *Toxocara canis* roundworm egg to himself passing viable eggs (the pre-patent period). These eggs are not immediately infective to other animals, requiring a period of maturation in the environment, which is primarily temperature dependent and therefore shorter in the summer (as little as two weeks) than in the winter. The eggs can survive in the environment for two years and more.

There are de-worming products that are active all the time, which will provide continuous protection when administered as often as directed. Otherwise, treating every month will, in effect, cut in before a dog could theoretically become a source of roundworm eggs to the general population.

All puppies should be routinely treated for roundworm.

HEARTWORM (DIROFILARIA IMMITIS)

Heartworm infection has been diagnosed in dogs all over the world. There are two prerequisites: the presence of mosquitoes and a warm, humid climate.

When a female mosquito bites an infected animal, it acquires *D. immitis* in its circulating form, as microfilariae. A warm environmental temperature is needed for these microfilariae to develop into the infective third-stage larvae (L3) within the mosquitoes, the so-called intermediate host. L3 larvae are then transmitted by the mosquito when it next bites a dog. Therefore, while heartworm infection is found in all parts of the United States, it is at differing levels. An occurrence in Alaska, for example, is probably a reflection of a visiting dog having previously picked up the infection elsewhere.

Heartworm infection is not currently a problem in the UK, except for those dogs contracting it while abroad without suitable preventative treatment. Global warming and its effect on the UK's climate, however, could change that.

It is a potentially life-threatening condition, with dogs of all breeds and ages being susceptible without preventative treatment. The larvae can grow to 14 inches within the right side of the heart, causing primarily signs of heart failure and ultimately liver and kidney damage. It can be treated, but prevention is a better plan. In the United States, regular blood tests for the presence of infection are advised, coupled with appropriate preventative measures, so I would advise liaison with your veterinary surgeon.

For dogs travelling to heartworm-endemic areas of the EU, such as the Mediterranean coast, preventative treatment should be started before leaving the UK and maintained during the visit. Again, this is best arranged with your vet.

It is the risk to human health that is so important: *Toxocara canis* roundworms will migrate within our tissues and cause all manner of problems, not least of which (but fortunately rarely) is blindness. If a dog has roundworms, the eggs also find their way on to his coat, where they can be picked up during stroking. Sensible hygiene is therefore important. You should always carefully pick up your dog's faeces and dispose of them appropriately, thereby preventing the maturation of any eggs present in the fresh faeces.

TAPEWORMS (CESTODES)

When considering the general dog population, the primary source of the commonest tapeworm species will be fleas, which can carry the eggs. Most multi-wormers will be active against these tapeworms. They are not a threat to human health, but it is unpleasant to see the wriggly ricegrain tapeworm segments emerging from your dog's back passage while he is lying in front of the fire, and usually when you have guests for dinner!

A tapeworm of significance to human health is **Echinococcus** *granulosus*, found in a few parts of the UK, mainly in Wales. Man is an intermediate host for this tapeworm, along with sheep, cattle and pigs. Inadvertent ingestion of eggs passed in the faeces of an infected dog is followed by the development of so-called hydatid cysts in major organs, such as the lungs and liver, necessitating surgical removal. Dogs become infected through eating raw meat containing hydatid cysts. Cooking will kill hydatid cysts, so avoid feeding raw meat and offal in areas of high risk.

There are specific

requirements for treatment with 'praziquantel' within 24 to 48 hours of return into the UK under the PETS. This is to prevent the inadvertent introduction of *Echinococcus multilocularis*, a tapeworm carried by foxes on mainland Europe which is transmissible to humans, causing serious or even fatal liver disease.

FLEAS

There are several species of flea, which are not host-specific. A dog can be carrying cat and human fleas as well as dog fleas, but the same flea treatment will kill and/or control them all. It is also accepted that environmental control is a vital part of a flea control programme. This is because the adult flea is only on the animal for as long as it takes to have a blood meal and to breed; the remainder of the life cycle occurs in the house, car, caravan, shed...

There is a vast array of flea control products available, with various routes of administration: collar, powder, spray, 'spot-on', or oral. Flea control needs to be applied to all pets in the house, regardless of whether they leave the house, since fleas can be introduced into the home by other pets and their human owners. Discuss your specific flea control needs with your vet.

MITES

There are five types of mite that can affect dogs:

Spot on treatment is an easy and effective method of preventing flea infestation.

Demodex canis: This mite is a normal inhabitant of canine hair follicles, passed from the bitch to her pups as they suckle. The development of actual skin disease or demodicosis depends on the individual. It is seen frequently around the time of puberty and after a bitch's first season, associated with hormonal changes. There may, however, be an inherited weakness in an individual's immune system, enabling multiplication of the mite.

The localised form consists of areas of fur loss without itchiness, generally around the face and on the forelimbs and 90 per cent will recover without treatment. The other 10 per cent develop the juvenile-onset generalised form, of which half

will recover spontaneously. The other half may be depressed, go off their food, and show signs of itchiness due to secondary bacterial skin infections.

Treatment is often prolonged over several months and consists of regular bathing with a specific miticidal shampoo, often clipping away fur to improve access to the skin, together with a suitable antibiotic by mouth. There is also now a licensed 'spot-on' preparation available. Progress is monitored by the examination of deep skin scrapings for the presence of the mite; the initial diagnosis is based upon abnormally high numbers of the mite, often with live individuals being seen.

Some Border Collies may develop demodicosis for the first

Dogs that are exercised in long grass are more likely to pick up ticks.

time in middle-age (more than four years of age). This often reflects underlying immunosuppression by an internal disease, so it is important to identify such a cause and correct it where possible, as well as treating the skin condition.

Sarcoptes scabei: This characteristically causes an intense pruritus or itchiness in the affected Border Collie, causing him to incessantly scratch and bite at himself, leading to marked fur loss and skin trauma. Initially starting on the elbows, earflaps and hocks, without treatment the skin on the rest of the body can become affected, with thickening and pigmentation of the skin. Secondary bacterial infections are common.

Unlike *Demodex*, this mite lives at the skin surface and it can be hard to find in skin scrapings. It is therefore not unusual to treat a patient for **sarcoptic mange (scabies)** based on the appearance of the problem, even with negative skin scraping findings and especially if there is a history of contact with foxes, which are a frequent source of the scabies mite.

It will spread between dogs and can therefore also be found in situations where large numbers of dogs from different backgrounds are mixing together. It will cause itchiness in humans, although the mite cannot complete its life cycle on us, so treating all affected dogs should be sufficient. Fortunately, there is now a highly effective 'spot-on' treatment for *Sarcoptes scabei*. Care must be taken to ensure there is not an exclusion

against use on the Border Collie, as there is with some products and that the dose given is based on an accurate current bodyweight in order to avoid over-dosage.

Cheyletiella yasguri: This is the fur mite most commonly found on dogs. It is often called 'walking dandruff', because it can be possible to see collections of the small white mite moving about over the skin surface. There is excessive scale and dandruff formation and mild itchiness. It is transmissible to humans, causing a pruritic rash.

Diagnosis is by microscopic examination of skin scrapings, coat combings and sticky tape impressions from the skin and fur. Treatment is with an appropriate insecticide, as advised by your veterinary surgeon.

Dogs are natural scavengers and this can lead to digestive upset.

Otodectes cynotis: A highly transmissible otitis externa (outer ear infection) results from the presence in the outer ear canal of the ear mite characterised by exuberant production of dark earwax. The patient will frequently shake his head and rub at the ear(s) affected. The mites can also spread on to the skin adjacent to the opening of the external ear canal and may transfer elsewhere, such as to the paws.

When using an otoscope to examine the outer ear canal, the heat from the light source will often cause any ear mites present to start moving around. I often offer owners the chance to have a look, because it really is quite an extraordinary sight! It is also possible to identify the mite from earwax smeared on to a slide and examined under a microscope.

Cats are a common source of ear mites. It is not unusual to find ear mites during the routine examination of puppies and kittens. Treatment options include specific eardrops acting against both the mite and any secondary infections present in the auditory canal, and certain 'spot-on' formulations. It is vital to treat all dogs and cats in the household to prevent recycling of the mite between individuals.

Trombicula autumnalis: The free-living mite (**Neo-**) or **harvest mite** can cause an intense local irritation on the skin. Its larvae are picked up from undergrowth, so they are characteristically found as a bright orange patch on the web of skin between the digits of the paws. It feeds on skin cells before dropping off to complete its life cycle in the environment.

Its name is a little misleading, because it is not restricted to the autumn nor to harvest-time; I find it on the earflaps of cats from late June onwards, depending on the prevailing weather. It will also bite humans.

Treatment depends on identifying and avoiding hotspots for picking up harvest mites, if possible. Checking the skin, especially the paws, after exercise and mechanically removing any mites found will reduce the chances of irritation, which can be treated symptomatically. Insecticides can also be applied – be guided by your veterinary surgeon.

TICKS
Ticks have become an increasing problem in recent years throughout Britain. Their

EAR INFECTIONS

The dog has a long external ear canal, initially vertical then horizontal, leading to the eardrum, which protects the middle ear. If your Border Collie is shaking his head, then his ears will need to be inspected with an auroscope by a veterinary surgeon in order to identify any cause and to ensure the eardrum is intact. A sample may be taken from the canal to be examined under the microscope and cultured, to identify causal agents before prescribing appropriate eardrops containing antibiotic, antifungal agent and/or steroid. Predisposing causes of otitis externa or infection in the external ear canal include:

- Presence of a foreign body, such as a grass awn
- Ear mites, which are intensely irritating to the dog and stimulate the production of brown wax, predisposing to infection
- Previous infections, causing the canal's lining to thicken, narrowing the canal and reducing ventilation
- Swimming – many Border Collies simply adore will swimming. I always knew winter had arrived when Nan, my first Border Collie, stopped taking her daily dip in the river! However, water trapped in the external ear canal can lead to infection, especially if the water is not clean.

physical presence causes irritation, but it is their potential to spread disease that causes concern. A tick will transmit any infection previously contracted while feeding on an animal: for example *Borrelia burgdorferi*, the causal agent of Lyme disease (see page 131).

The life cycle of the tick is curious: each life stage takes a year to develop and move on to the next. Long grass is a major habitat. The vibration of animals moving through the grass will stimulate the larva, nymph or adult to climb up a blade of grass and wave its legs in the air as it 'quests' for a host on to which to latch for its next blood meal.

Humans are as likely to be hosts, so ramblers and orienteers are advised to cover their legs when going through rough long grass.

Removing a tick is simple – provided your dog will stay still. The important rule is to twist gently so that the tick is persuaded to let go with its mouthparts. Grasp the body of the tick as near to your dog's skin as possible, either between thumb and fingers or with a specific tick-removing instrument and then rotate in one direction until the tick comes away. I keep a plastic tick hook in my wallet at all times so I can remove ticks as soon as I notice them.

A-Z OF COMMON AILMENTS

IMPACTED ANAL SACS

The anal sacs lie on either side of the anus at approximately four and eight o'clock, if compared with the face of a clock. They fill with a particularly pungent fluid, which is emptied on to the faeces as they move past the sacs to exit from the anus. Theories abound as to why these sacs should become impacted periodically and seemingly more so in some dogs than others.

The irritation of impacted anal sacs is often seen as 'scooting', when the backside is dragged

The Border Collie needs to be kept in lean, fit condition.

along the ground. Some dogs will also gnaw at their back feet or over the rump.

Increasing the fibre content of the diet helps some dogs; in others, there is underlying skin disease. It may be a one-off occurrence for no apparent reason. Sometimes an infection can become established, requiring antibiotic therapy, which may need to be coupled with flushing out the infected sac under sedation or general anaesthesia. More rarely, a dog will present with an apparently acute-onset anal sac abscess, which is incredibly painful.

DIARRHOEA
Cause and treatment much as **Gastritis** (see below).

FOREIGN BODIES
Internal: Items swallowed in haste without checking whether they will be digested can cause problems if they lodge in the stomach or obstruct the intestines, necessitating surgical removal. Acute vomiting is the main indication. Common objects I have seen removed include; stones from the garden, peach stones, babies' dummies, golf balls and once, a lady's bra...

It is possible to diagnose a dog with an intestinal obstruction across a waiting room from a particularly 'tucked-up' stance and pained facial expression. These patients bounce back from surgery dramatically. A previously docile and compliant obstructed patient will return for a post-operative check-up and literally bounce into the consulting room.

External: Grass awns are adept at finding their way into orifices such as a nostril, down an ear and into the soft skin between two digits (toes), whence they start a one-way journey due to the direction of their whiskers. In particular, I remember a grass awn that migrated from a hind paw, causing abscesses along the way, but not yielding itself up until it erupted through the skin in the groin!

GASTRITIS
This is usually a simple stomach upset, most commonly in response to dietary indiscretion. In the case of a Border Collie, garbage gastritis is an even better description because they are a breed clever enough to be constantly on the look out for edible matter, either during a walk or opportunistically within the home environment, such as the kitchen waste bin! Scavenging constitutes a change in the diet as much as an abrupt switch in the food being fed by the owner.

There are also some specific infections causing more severe gastritis/enteritis, which will require treatment from a veterinary surgeon (see also **Canine Parvovirus** under

OBESITY

Being overweight does predispose to many other problems, such as diabetes mellitus, heart disease and joint problems. It is so easily prevented by simply acting as your Border Collie's conscience. Ignore pleading eyes and feed according to your dog's waistline. The body condition is what matters qualitatively, alongside monitoring that individual's bodyweight as a quantitative measure. The Border Collie should, in my opinion as a health professional, have at least a suggestion of a waist and it should be possible to feel the ribs beneath only a slight layer of fat.

Neutering does not automatically mean that your Border Collie will be overweight. Having an ovario-hysterectomy does slow down the body's rate of working, castration to a lesser extent, but it therefore means that your dog needs less food. I recommend cutting back a little on the amount of food fed a few weeks before neutering, to accustom your Border Collie to less food. If she looks a little underweight on the morning of the operation, it will help the veterinary surgeon as well as giving her a little leeway weight-wise afterwards. It is always harder to lose weight after neutering than before, because of this slowing in the body's inherent metabolic rate.

'Vaccination' on page 127).

Generally, a day without food, followed by a few days of small, frequent meals of a bland diet (such as cooked chicken or fish), or an appropriate prescription diet, should allow the stomach to settle. It is vital to ensure the patient is drinking and retaining sufficient water to cover losses resulting from the stomach upset, in addition to the normal losses to be expected when healthy. Oral rehydration fluid may not be very appetising for the patient, in which case cooled boiled water should be offered. Fluids should initially be offered in small but frequent amounts to avoid over-drinking, which can result in further vomiting and thereby dehydration and electrolyte imbalances. It is also important to wean the patient back on to routine food gradually, or else another bout of gastritis may occur.

JOINT PROBLEMS (SEE ALSO INHERITED DISORDERS)

It is not unusual for older Border Collies to be stiff after exercise, particularly in cold weather and especially if coupled with a swim. This is not really surprising, given that they are such busy dogs when young. This is such a game naturally active breed that a nine or ten-year-old Border Collie will not readily forego an extra walk or take kindly to turning for home earlier than usual. Your veterinary surgeon will be able to advise you on ways of helping your dog cope with stiffness, not least of which will be to ensure that he is not overweight. Arthritic joints do not need to be burdened with extra bodyweight!

LUMPS

Regularly handling and stroking your Border Collie will enable the early detection of lumps and bumps. These may be due to infection (abscess), bruising, multiplication of particular cells from within the body, or even an external parasite (tick). If you are worried about any lump you find, have it checked by a vet.

The Border Collie seems to be predisposed to developing fatty lumps (lipomata). Sometimes, their sheer size coupled with the position on the body may cause problems, or if they grow and spread into surrounding tissues.

Mammary tumours are also relatively common and should be checked by a veterinary surgeon as soon as they are found.

MOULTING

Having been brought up with Border Collies who lived indoors with us as part of the family, I know all too well just how much fur they shed. The trouble is that we humans seek to maintain a constant non-seasonal environment within our homes, which confuses the Border Collie into seemingly moulting all year round! Regular grooming should help keep things in check. Those kennelled outside will experience the seasons as they are meant to be and should simply moult as appropriate, although still needing to be groomed.

TEETH

Eating food starts with the canine teeth gripping and killing prey in the wild, incisor teeth biting off pieces of food and the molar teeth chewing it. To be able to eat is vital for life, yet the actual health of the teeth is often overlooked: unhealthy teeth can predispose to disease and not just by reducing the ability to eat. The presence of infection within the mouth can lead to bacteria entering the bloodstream and then filtering out at major organs, with the potential for serious consequences. That is not to forget that simply having dental

Fortunately, there is a low incidence of inherited disorders in Border Collies.

pain can affect a dog's wellbeing, as anyone who has had toothache will confirm.

The Border Collie loves retrieving games. So-called pharyngeal stick injuries are a classic consequence of chasing a stick which has been thrown as a retrieve article: jumping on to the stick in the process of picking it up can cause damage within the mouth and splinters driven deep into the tissues may cause recurrent infections. As vets, we advise against throwing sticks and instead suggest having suitable toys on your person for your Border Collie to retrieve while out on a walk. But they will often still carry sticks and even great big logs, which may result in worn and broken teeth. Eating stones, a habit some dogs have, will also damage the teeth.

Veterinary dentistry has made huge leaps in recent years, so that it no longer consists of

extraction as the treatment of necessity. Good dental health lies in the hands of the owner, starting from the moment the dog comes into your care. Just as we have taken on responsibility for feeding, so we have acquired the task of maintaining good dental and oral hygiene. In an ideal world, we should brush our dogs' teeth as regularly as our own, but the Border Collie puppy who finds having his teeth brushed is a huge game and an excuse to roll over and over on the ground, requires loads of patience, twice a day.

There are alternative strategies, ranging from dental chewsticks to specially formulated foods, but the main thing is to be aware of your dog's mouth. At least train your puppy to permit full examination of his teeth. This will not only ensure you are checking in his mouth regularly,

It is essential that dogs are screened before being used in a breeding programme.

but will also make your veterinary surgeon's job easier when there is a real need for your dog to 'open wide!'

INHERITED DISORDERS

Any individual, dog or human, may have an inherited disorder by virtue of the genes acquired from the parents. This is significant not only for the health of that individual, but also because of the potential for transmitting the disorder on to that individual's offspring and to subsequent generations, depending on the mode of inheritance.

There are control schemes in place for some inherited disorders. In the United States for example, the Canine Eye Registration Foundation (CERF) was set up by dog breeders concerned about heritable eye disease, and provides a database

of dogs who have been examined by diplomates of the American College of Veterinary Ophthalmologists.

As well as screening programmes, it is now possible to directly identify the genes responsible for certain inherited disorders. This means that, by running DNA tests before breeding, individuals carrying unwanted genes can be excluded from breeding programmes from the outset. All that is required is a blood sample and/or a cheek swab, depending on the condition being assessed. Both procedures are generally well tolerated.

Historically, the Border Collie is a working dog which has been bred to cope with the rigours of working with livestock on all manner of terrain whatever the weather. The incidence of inherited disease in the breed is

therefore low. Major inherited disorders of concern in the Border Collie include the following.

CATARACT

A cataract is a cloudiness of the lens of the eye. In the Border Collie, this is the developmental form of hereditary cataract, occurring in the middle-aged dog, rather than the congenital form seen in other breeds (where some form of lens opacity is present from birth). Inheritance has not been proven, so it is controlled under Schedule B of the BVA/KC/ISDS Scheme** in the UK, CERF in the United States.

CENTRAL PROGRESSIVE RETINAL ATROPHY (CPRA)

Also known as Retinal Pigment Epithelial Dystrophy (RPED), this condition results in

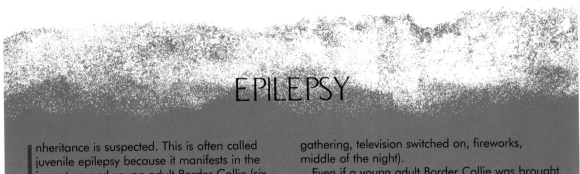

EPILEPSY

nheritance is suspected. This is often called juvenile epilepsy because it manifests in the immature and young adult Border Collie (six months to three years old), with convulsions occurring singly or in clusters.

It is very alarming as an owner to see your dog having a fit, because you feel utterly helpless. It is vital to note on a calendar or in a diary when a fit or cluster of fits occurs, together with information about concurrent happenings (for example; family gathering, television switched on, fireworks, middle of the night).

Even if a young adult Border Collie was brought to see me having had just one fit, I would be unlikely to start medication at once because 'every dog is allowed one or two fits'. Once medication has started, then one may never know whether or not he would have had any more fits at all. If it is needed to control the fits then medication will, from the nature of the problem, be life-long.

progressive damage to the retina, leading to a gradual loss in the central field of vision. As peripheral vision is maintained, many dogs show no signs of being affected.

CPRA is included in Schedule A of the BVA/KC/ISDS Scheme** in the UK, CERF in the United States.

CEROID LIPOFUSCINOSIS (CL)

This distressing condition, a lysosomal storage disease, is fortunately very rare. From early adulthood there is a progression of neurological signs from abnormal behaviour and altered gait, culminating in dementia and blindness. Fortunately, it is now possible to characterise individuals as clear, carrier or affected by submitting a blood sample to The Animal Health Trust in Newmarket in the UK for DNA testing, in order to avoid passing on the trait inadvertently.

COLLIE EYE ANOMALY/ CHOROIDAL HYPOPLASIA (CEA/CH)

This congenital disorder affects various parts of the eye (in particular, the retinal area). The affected areas do not develop normally. The severity of the disease ranges from mild visual impairment through to complete blindness. Affected dogs normally have only mildly impaired vision.

As with Central Progressive Retinal Atrophy, CEA/CH is controlled under Schedule A of the BVA/KC/ISDS Scheme** in the UK, CERF in the United States. There is also a DNA test available.

CONGENITAL DEAFNESS

This may be detected by the alert breeder very early on in a Border Collie puppy's life, from differences in behaviour when compared with the other members of the litter. Deafness is more frequently in one ear than in both and attributes seeming to be linked with deafness include; the merle coat colouring, blue pigment in the iris of the eye and a predominance of white fur on the head.

It is now possible to accurately assess a puppy's hearing from the age of five weeks, using the 'Brainstem Auditory Evoked Response' test, which is completely painless.

HIP DYSPLASIA

This is a malformation of the hip joints causing pain, lameness

TRAPPED NEUTROPHIL SYNDROME

This inherited disease of the immune system has become apparent in breeding lines which are only distantly related and in widely separated countries (UK, Australia, New Zealand), suggesting that it has actually been present for many generations. It has only recently come to prominence because until now it has been hard to recognise as a distinct problem. This is because it manifests in different ways between litters, often presenting simply as 'fading puppy syndrome'. Other signs are recurrent infections in young pups, or an adverse reaction at vaccination. Others may show few signs and live for several years.

It shows a recessive pattern of inheritance. Fortunately, a DNA test is now available for samples submitted to the University of New South Wales, Australia.

and reduced exercise tolerance in the young Border Collie and resulting in degenerative joint disease (arthritis) in the older dog. Each hip joint is scored on several features to give a total score of zero to 53 from a radiograph taken with the hips and pelvis in a specified position, usually requiring the dog to be sedated, after the age of one year under the BVA/KC Scheme* and from two years of age in the United States (OFA***).

OSTEOCHONDROSIS OF THE SHOULDER JOINTS

Affected individuals are more often male than female. A forelimb lameness tends to become apparent in the adolescent, although onset may on occasion be later. The diagnosis can be confirmed with radiographs.

PRIMARY LENS LUXATION (PLL)

In this condition, the lens of the eye separates from its attachments and moves either forwards or backwards in the eye. If the lens moves forwards, it can interfere with the drainage of fluid from the eye, which can lead to glaucoma. PLL can result from trauma as well as being inherited.

PLL can be treated very succesfully if it is diagnosed early enough. Like CPRA and CEA, Primary Lens Luxation is controlled under Schedule A of the BVA/KC/ISDS Scheme** in the UK, CERF in the United States.

*British Veterinary Association/Kennel Club Scheme
** British Veterinary Association/Kennel Club/International Sheepdog Society Scheme
***Orthopedic Foundation for Animals, United States

COMPLEMENTARY THERAPIES

Just as for human health, I do believe that there is a place for alternative therapies alongside and complementing orthodox treatment under the supervision of a veterinary surgeon. That is why 'complementary therapies' is a better name.

Because animals do not have a choice, there are measures in place to safeguard their wellbeing and welfare. All manipulative treatment must be under the direction of a veterinary surgeon who has examined the patient and diagnosed the condition that he or she feels needs that form of treatment. This covers physiotherapy, chiropractic, osteopathy and swimming therapy. For example, dogs with arthritis who cannot exercise as freely as they were accustomed will enjoy the sensation of controlled non-weight-bearing exercise in water and will benefit with improved muscling and overall fitness.

All other complementary therapies such as acupuncture, homoeopathy and aromatherapy, can only be carried out by veterinary surgeons who have been trained in that particular field. **Acupuncture** is mainly used in dogs for pain relief, often to good effect. The needles look more alarming to the owner, but they are very fine and are well tolerated by most canine patients. Speaking personally, superficial needling is not unpleasant and does help with pain relief. **Homoeopathy** has had a mixed press in recent years. It is based on the concept of treating like with like. Additionally, a homoeopathic remedy is said to become more powerful the more it is diluted.

SUMMARY
As the owner of a Border Collie, you are responsible for his care and health. Not only must you make decisions on his behalf, you are also responsible for establishing a lifestyle for him that will ensure he leads a long and happy life. Diet plays as

There is a growing awareness of the benefits of complementary therapies.

important a part in this, as does exercise.

For the domestic dog, it is only in recent years that the need has been recognised for changing the diet to suit the dog as he grows, matures and then enters his twilight years. So-called life-stage diets try to match the nutritional needs of the dog as he progresses through life.

An active or working dog food will suit the Border Collie working for his keep on a farm, but not those living a more sedentary life as part of the family. An adult dog food will suit the Border Collie living a standard family life. There are also foods for those Border Collies tactfully termed as obese-prone, such as those who have been neutered or are less active than others, or simply like their food. Do remember, though, that ultimately you are in control of

your Border Collie's diet, unless he is able to profit from scavenging!

On the other hand, prescription diets are of necessity fed under the supervision of a veterinary surgeon, because each is formulated to meet the very specific needs of particular health conditions. Should a prescription diet be fed to a healthy dog, or to a dog with a different illness, there could be adverse effects.

It is important to remember that your Border Collie has no choice. As his owner, you are responsible for any decision made, so it must be as informed a decision as possible. Always speak to your veterinary surgeon if you have any worries about your Border Collie. He is not just a dog; from the moment you brought him home, he became a member of the family.

THE CONTRIBUTORS

THE EDITOR
JUDITH GREGORY (TONKORY)

Judith Gregory has owned Border Collies for 50 years. She has worked them in obedience, agility and on sheep, but now concentrates on showing in breed competitions.

Judith has been the Top Breeder in the UK for five of the last six years and has been the top breeder in the Netherlands and other European countries. She bred the Border Collie Breed Record holder Sh Ch Tonkory Palmerston at Fayken JW, owned by Ross and Vicky Green, who has 45 CCs. Judith has bred ten show champions in the UK and five champions abroad. Judith judged Border Collie bitches at Crufts 2007.

A founder member and president of the West of England Border Collie Club, past acting chair and vice chair of the Border Collie Club of Great Britain and a member of the Border Collie Breed Council since its formation, she is currently the Border Collie Breed representative to the Kennel Club.

Her husband Dr John Gregory shares her interest in Border collies and is a committee member of the WOEBCC and acts as Show Manager in their shows throughout the year. He looks after the dogs whilst Judith is away showing and has also been very supportive and helpful with the editing of this book.
See Chapter One: Getting to Know the Border Collie; Chapter Three: A Border Collie for your Lifestyle; Chapter Seven: The Perfect Border Collie.

GEOFF AND FIONA PATON
(WILLIANWAYS)

Geoff and Fiona Paton are Scots who now live in Norfolk with their six border collies. Geoff is an engineering graduate who took early retirement from an international career in product design and development. He is a low handicap golfer and a qualified dog show judge specialising in border collies. Fiona has owned and loved various breeds of dogs throughout her life. She is a published freelance writer and a keen genealogist.

Geoff and Fiona acquired their first border collie in 1992 and he introduced them to the world of agility, obedience and eventually the show scene. They show their dogs lightly but with some success under the kennel name "Willianways". Two bitches

bred at Locheil by Heather Turner have been particularly successful, each having won a class at Crufts. Two lovely litters have been born at Willianways.

Geoff and Fiona have travelled extensively and enjoyed dog shows in the USA and Australia. It is their particular pleasure to watch National and International Sheepdog Trials. Their enthusiasm for border collies has led to the collection of an extensive library on breed history and a large computer database of key dogs.
See Chapter Two: The First Border Collies; Chapter Five: The Best of Care.

PAM HARRIS

Pam Harris has been breeding dogs for more than 45 years. Pam met her late husband, Alan, at obedience training classes. Shortly after they married, Alan purchased a Border Collie to train and so began their life-long love of the breed.

Pam and Alan bred Ob. Ch. Mobella Ryley (owned by Terry Hannam) and also Mobella Jez (owned by the late Neville Johnson) who won two obedience CCs.

When Border Collies were recognised by the Kennel Club, Pam and Alan began showing them in breed classes. Over the years Pam has bred and shown many Champion Border Collies. One of Pam's proudest achievements was breeding Sh. Ch. Mobella Team Spirit at Tonkory, who proved to be an outstanding dam.

Pam was Top Breeder in the UK in 1995. She also judges Border Collies at Championship show level.
See Chapter Four: The New Arrival.

JULIA BARNES

Julia has owned and trained a number of different dog breeds, and is a puppy socialiser for Dogs for the Disabled. A former journalist, she has written many books, including several on dog training and behaviour. Julia is indebted to Rose Bugler for her specialist knowledge of Border Collies.
See Chapter Six: Training and Socialisation

ROSE BUGLER

Rose Bugler is the Director of the DVD "Well Balanced Pup" which follows 5 litters of Border Collies over their first eight weeks showing socialisation tips and techniques to

make sure the puppies get the best possible start in life. Many of the dogs shown in the DVD have gone on to success in agility and obedience, search and rescue, working sheep dogs and become well loved family pets, demonstrating the versatility of a well bred and well trained Border Collie. The DVD emphasises the importance of the health and temperament of the parents of any puppies bred as well as demonstrating ways in which many of the behavioral difficulties seen in dogs who have needed re-homing can be avoided by careful breeding and rearing. The DVD also features dogs being trained as search and rescue dogs for SARDA Lakes as well as some showing agility dogs in action. Rose owns 2 Border Collies and a Springer-Collie cross and is training them for agility and geese herding.

The DVD can be bought through their website www.wellbalancedpup.co.uk or they can be contacted on 07876 363668.

ALISON LOGAN MA VetMB MRCVS

Alison qualified as a veterinary surgeon from Cambridge University in 1989, having been brought up surrounded by all manner of animals and birds in the north Essex countryside. She has been in practice in her home town ever since, living with her husband, two children and Labrador Retriever.

She contributes on a regular basis to *Veterinary Times, Veterinary Nurse Times, Dogs Today, Cat World* and *Pet Patter*, the PetPlan newsletter. In 1995, Alison won the Univet Literary Award with an article on Cushing's Disease, and she won it again (as the Vetoquinol Literary Award) in 2002, writing about common conditions in the Shar-Pei.
See Chapter Eight: Happy and Healthy.

LAKE DISTRICT SHEEPDOG EXPERIENCE

The Lake District Sheep Dog Experience provides an instructional Border Collie sheepdog handling experience. Based on a Lake District hill farm, farming the traditional Herdwick sheep, in the stunning Duddon valley area, between Langdale, Eskdale, Coniston and Broughton, visitors can themselves experience handling one of their friendly and fully trained sheepdogs under instruction. Visit their website:
www.lakedistrictsheepdogexperience.co.uk

USEFUL ADDRESSES

KENNEL & BREED CLUBS

UK
The Kennel Club
1-5 Clarges Street, London, W1J 8AB
Tel: 0870 606 6750
Fax: 0207 518 1058
Web: www.the-kennel-club.org.uk

To obtain up-to-date contact information for the following breed clubs, contact the Kennel Club:
• Border Collie Club of Great Britain
• Border Collie Club of Wales
• East Anglian Border Collie Club
• Midlands Border Collie Club
• North West Border Collie Club
• Scottish Border Collie Club
• Southern Border Collie Club
• West of England Border Collie Club
• Wessex Border Collie Club.

USA
American Kennel Club (AKC)
5580 Centerview Drive, Raleigh, NC 27606, USA.
Tel: 919 233 9767
Fax: 919 233 3627
Email: info@akc.org
Web: www.akc.org

United Kennel Club (UKC)
100 E Kilgore Rd, Kalamazoo,
MI 49002-5584, USA.
Tel: 269 343 9020
Fax: 269 343 7037
Web:www.ukcdogs.com/

Border Collie Society of America, Inc.
Web: http://www.bordercolliesociety.com/

For contact details of regional clubs, please contact the Border Collie Society of America.

AUSTRALIA
Australian National Kennel Council (ANKC)
The Australian National Kennel Council is the administrative body for pure breed canine affairs in Australia. It does not, however, deal directly with dog exhibitors, breeders or judges. For information pertaining to breeders, clubs or shows, please contact the relevant State or Territory Controlling Body.

Dogs Australian Capital Teritory
PO Box 815, Dickson ACT 2602
Tel: (02) 6241 4404
Fax: (02) 6241 1129
Email: administrator@dogsact.org.au
Web: www.dogsact.org.au

Dogs New South Wales
PO Box 632, St Marys, NSW 1790
Tel: (02) 9834 3022 or 1300 728 022
Fax: (02) 9834 3872
Email: info@dogsnsw.org.au
Web: www.dogsnsw.org.au

Dogs Northern Territory
PO Box 37521, Winnellie NT 0821
Tel: (08) 8984 3570
Fax: (08) 8984 3409
Email: admin@dogsnt.com.au
Web: www.dogsnt.com.au

Dogs Queensland
PO Box 495, Fortitude Valley Qld 4006
Tel: (07) 3252 2661
Fax: (07) 3252 3864
Email: info@dogsqueensland.org.au
Web: www.dogsqueensland.org.au

Dogs South Australia
PO Box 844
Prospect East SA 5082
Tel: (08) 8349 4797
Fax: (08) 8262 5751
Email: info@dogssa.com.au
Web: www.dogssa.com.au

Tasmanian Canine Association Inc
The Rothman Building
PO Box 116, Glenorchy Tas 7010
Tel: (03) 6272 9443
Fax: (03) 6273 0844
Email: tca@iprimus.com.au
Web: www.tasdogs.com

Dogs Victoria
Locked Bag K9
Cranbourne VIC 3977
Tel: (03)9788 2500
Fax: (03) 9788 2599
Email: office@dogsvictoria.org.au
Web: www.dogsvictoria.org.au

Dogs Western Australia
PO Box 1404 Canning Vale WA 6970
Tel: (08) 9455 1188
Fax: (08) 9455 1190
Email: k9@dogswest.com
Web: www.dogswest.com

INTERNATIONAL
Fédération Cynologique Internationalé (FCI)/World Canine Organisation
Place Albert 1er, 13, B-6530 Thuin,
Belgium.
Tel: +32 71 59.12.38
Fax: +32 71 59.22.29
Web: www.fci.be/

TRAINING AND BEHAVIOUR

UK
Association of Pet Dog Trainers
PO Box 17, Kempsford, GL7 4WZ
Telephone: 01285 810811
Email: APDToffice@aol.com
Web: http://www.apdt.co.uk

Association of Pet Behaviour Counsellors
PO BOX 46, Worcester, WR8 9YS
Telephone: 01386 751151
Fax: 01386 750743
Email: info@apbc.org.uk
Web: http://www.apbc.org.uk/

USA
Association of Pet Dog Trainers
101 North Main Street, Suite 610
Greenville, SC 29601, USA.
Tel: 1 800 738 3647
Email: information@apdt.com
Web: www.apdt.com/

American College of Veterinary Behaviorists
College of Veterinary Medicine, 4474 Tamu,
Texas A&M University
College Station, Texas 77843-4474
Web: http://dacvb.org/

American Veterinary Society of Animal Behavior
Web: www.avsabonline.org/

AUSTRALIA
APDT Australia Inc
PO Box 3122, Bankstown Square, NSW 2200,
Email: secretary@apdt.com.au
Web: www.apdt.com.au

Canine Behaviour
For details of regional behvaiourists, contact the relevant State or Territory Controlling Body.

ACTIVITIES

UK
Agility Club
http://www.agilityclub.co.uk/

British Flyball Association
PO Box 990, Doncaster, DN1 9FY
Telephone: 01628 829623
Email: secretary@flyball.org.uk
Web: http://www.flyball.org.uk/

Working Trials
www.workingtrials.co.uk

USA
North American Dog Agility Council
P.O. Box 1206, Colbert,
OK 74733, USA.
Web: www.nadac.com/

North American Flyball Association, Inc.
1333 West Devon Avenue, #512
Chicago, IL 60660
Tel/Fax: 800 318 6312
Email: flyball@flyball.org
Web: www.flyball.org/

Agility Dog Association of Australia
ADAA Secretary, PO Box 2212,
Gailes, QLD 4300, Australia.
Tel: 0423 138 914
Email: admin@adaa.com.au
Web: www.adaa.com.au/

NADAC Australia (North American Dog Agility Council - Australian Division)
12 Wellman Street, Box Hill South, Victoria 3128, Australia.
Email: shirlene@nadacaustralia.com
Web: www.nadacaustralia.com/

Australian Flyball Association
PO Box 4179, Pitt Town, NSW 2756
Tel: 0407 337 939
Email: info@flyball.org.au
Web: www.flyball.org.au/

INTERNATIONAL

World Canine Freestyle Organisation
P.O. Box 350122, Brooklyn, NY 11235-2525, USA
Tel: (718) 332-8336
Fax: (718) 646-2686
Email: wcfodogs@aol.com
Web: www.worldcaninefreestyle.org

HEALTH

UK

Alternative Veterinary Medicine Centre
Chinham House, Stanford in the Vale,
Oxfordshire, SN7 8NQ
Tel: 01367 710324
Fax: 01367 718243
Web: www.alternativevet.org/

British Small Animal Veterinary Association
Woodrow House, 1 Telford Way,
Waterwells Business Park, Quedgeley,
Gloucestershire, GL2 2AB
Tel: 01452 726700
Fax: 01452 726701
Email: customerservices@bsava.com
Web: http://www.bsava.com/

Royal College of Veterinary Surgeons
Belgravia House, 62-64 Horseferry Road, London,
SW1P 2AF
Tel: 0207 222 2001
Fax: 0207 222 2004
Email: admin@rcvs.org.uk
Web: www.rcvs.org.uk

USA

American Holistic Veterinary Medical Association
2218 Old Emmorton Road
Bel Air, MD 21015

Tel: 410 569 0795
Fax 410 569 2346
Email: office@ahvma.org
Web: www.ahvma.org/

American Veterinary Medical Association
1931 North Meacham Road, Suite 100,
Schaumburg, IL 60173-4360, USA.
Tel: 800 248 2862
Fax: 847 925 1329
Web: www.avma.org

American College of Veterinary Surgeons
19785 Crystal Rock Dr, Suite 305
Germantown, MD 20874, USA.
Tel: 301 916 0200
Toll Free: 877 217 2287
Fax: 301 916 2287
Email: acvs@acvs.org
Web: www.acvs.org/

AUSTRALIA
Australian Holistic Vets
Web: www.ahv.com.au/

Australian Small Animal Veterinary Association
40/6 Herbert Street, St Leonards, NSW 2065
Tel: 02 9431 5090
Fax: 02 9437 9068
Email: asava@ava.com.au
Web: www.asava.com.au

Australian Veterinary Association
Unit 40, 6 Herbert Street, St Leonards, NSW
2065, Australia.
Tel: 02 9431 5000
Fax: 02 9437 9068
Web: www.ava.com.au

Australian College Veterinary Scientists
Building 3, Garden City Office Park,
2404 Logan Road, Eight Mile Plains, Queensland
4113, Australia.
Tel: 07 3423 2016
Fax: 07 3423 2977
Email: admin@acvs.org.au
Web: http://acvsc.org.au

ASSISTANCE DOGS

UK
Canine Partners
Mill Lane, Heyshott, Midhurst, GU29 0ED
Tel: 08456 580480
Fax: 08456 580481
Web: www.caninepartners.co.uk

Dogs for the Disabled
The Frances Hay Centre, Blacklocks Hill,
Banbury, Oxon, OX17 2BS
Tel: 01295 252600
Web: www.dogsforthedisabled.org

Guide Dogs for the Blind Association
Burghfield Common, Reading, RG7 3YG
Tel: 01189 835555
Fax: 01189 835433
Web: www.guidedogs.org.uk/

Hearing Dogs for Deaf People
The Grange, Wycombe Road, Saunderton, Princes
Risborough, Bucks, HP27 9NS
Tel: 01844 348100
Fax: 01844 348101
Web: www.hearingdogs.org.uk

Pets as Therapy
14a High Street, Wendover, Aylesbury, Bucks.
HP22 6EA.
Tel: 01845 345445
Fax: 01845 550236
Web: http://www.petsastherapy.org/

Support Dogs
21 Jessops Riverside, Brightside Lane, Sheffield, S9
2RX
Tel: 01142 617800
Fax: 01142 617555
Email: supportdogs@btconnect.com
Web: www.support-dogs.org.uk

USA
Therapy Dogs International
88 Bartley Road, Flanders, NJ 07836,.
Tel: 973 252 9800
Fax: 973 252 7171
Web: www.tdi-dog.o

Therapy Dogs Inc.
P.O. Box 20227, Cheyenne, WY 82003.
Tel: 307 432 0272.
Fax: 307-638-2079
Web: www.therapydogs.com

Delta Society - Pet Partners
875 124th Ave NE, Suite 101, Bellevue, WA
98005 USA.
Email: info@DeltaSociety.org
Web: www.deltasociety.org

Comfort Caring Canines
8135 Lare Street, Philadelphia, PA 19128.
Email: ccc@comfortcaringcanines.org
Web: www.comfortcaringcanines.org/

AUSTRALIA
AWARE Dogs Australia, Inc
PO Box 883, Kuranda, Queensland, 488..
Tel: 07 4093 8152
Web: www.awaredogs.org.au/

Delta Society — Therapy Dogs
Web: www.deltasociety.com.au